Cordial Relations between Africa and America in the Twenty-First Century

How the United States Can Help to Transform the Continent

LAZARUS JAWIYAMBE

CORDIAL RELATIONS BETWEEN AFRICA AND
AMERICA IN THE TWENTY-FIRST CENTURY
HOW THE UNITED STATES CAN HELP TO
TRANSFORM THE CONTINENT

iUniverse books may be ordered through booksellers or by contacting:

iUniverse
1663 Liberty Drive
Bloomington, IN 47403
www.iuniverse.com
1-800-Authors (1-800-288-4677)

ISBN: 978-1-5320-4287-4 (sc)
ISBN: 978-1-5320-4286-7 (e)

Library of Congress Control Number: 2018902007

Print information available on the last page.

iUniverse rev. date: 03/19/2018

To all those who have traveled the long journey with me: Chance, Grant, Omani, Eliza, Hawa, and Aryo

Contents

Introduction

Cordial Relations between Africa and the United States in the Twenty-First Century: How the United States Can Help to Transform the Continent is about a new partnership between the people of the United States and the people of the ancient continent of Africa—a friendship based on complete trust and an understanding of each side's weaknesses and important national interests. The US-African relationship has been marked by so much mistrust and so many missteps that African nations have come to prefer dealing with other powers, such as the former Soviet Union, the European Union, and of course today China.

The main reason for writing *Cordial Relations between Africa and the United States in the Twenty-First Century* is to help enhance the cooperation between Africa and the United States now and for years to come. The United States, as the senior partner and more developed country with many resources, should generously help the people of Africa to transform their nations.

For the first time in many decades, a large number of young Africans are cautiously optimistic about their prospects in the region. This is because of the changing circumstances and opportunities in the continent. It is true that many countries in the region are still struggling with the challenges of economic underdevelopment and bad governance. However, there are also very hopeful signs of sustained economic growth and good leadership.

Young people, and indeed other Africans, are seeing the developments and are choosing to participate in the creation of a new Africa. For example, in Uganda, President Yoweri Museveni is encouraging and actively working with young professionals to initiate a wide range of small businesses.

This is exactly the kind of leadership Africa has been lacking. In some countries, educated young people are behind the high-tech start-ups now taking shape, with very promising results.

Now, whether or not all these developments will significantly improve the prospects of the majority of African nations, only time will tell. But I strongly believe that things are turning around for the better in countries such as Rwanda, Uganda, Kenya, Tanzania, South Africa, Botswana, and Senegal. And it is for this reason that the United States should lend more support to the region.

The United States has experience with helping nations turn their misfortunes into prospects. It did so in Europe, Japan, and other places after the Second World War. And the same is possible in Africa—if there is the will to make it happen.

Africans and the people of the United States must look past the difficulties that have characterized their relationship, especially as a result of the Cold War. Let both sides look at where things went wrong and learn from the experience—in the interests of furthering cordial cooperation.

1

Post–Cold War Relations

When the historic Gorbachev era began in the USSR at the height of the Cold War, Africa was not spared the devastating impact of the rivalry between Gorbachev's country and the USA. As a result, Cold War thinking completely defined and dominated the USA's foreign policy attitude toward African nations, regardless of the international priorities and intentions of these poor and weak countries. Consequently, post–Cold War relations between the United States and African countries continued to be severely strained exactly because the United States would not allow itself to positively view the African situation as a struggle for national independence and self-respect.

Other significant reasons made relations less smooth and less constructive between Africa and the United States—for example, the lingering suspicions that the United States did not really care about Africa because of racial differences and the fact that people of the United States, just like the Europeans, were still bent on imperial domination and mainly interested in the exploitation of Africa's vast natural resources. This line of thinking was leveraged by the old guard leaders in sub-Saharan Africa, who strongly resisted all Western intentions for the continent. Not all US or other Western nations' intentions and policies were bad for Africa. However, within the poisonous atmosphere of the post–Cold War era, any move, especially by the United States, aroused suspicions by the Africans and was at worst rejected—even before such moves were properly examined.

These and many other differences between the United States and Africa continued to push some African nations toward the Soviet bloc, although mainly for strategic and tactical reasons. Africans were looking to Moscow or China not for communism but for economic, political, and military assistance, without strings or humiliating conditions attached. The African leaders of the time benefited politically from the relationships with the communist nations, but their citizens did not. The tyrannical African leaders knew that the Soviet bloc and China cared less than the United States about human rights abuses, corruption, bad governance, lack of democracy, and so forth, all of which prevailed in most of sub-Saharan Africa.

However, as Mikhail Gorbachev started to introduce major reforms into the Soviet political system in the 1980s in what came to be known as perestroika, the impact of the changes went far beyond the borders of the Soviet bloc to the countries of Africa. As Gorbachev pushed forward with reforming the heavily outdated system in that huge empire, the USSR soon started to crack from within, and the country started to retreat internationally. This meant the beginning of the abandonment of traditional military, economic, and political alliances and of the USSR's commitments to its client states and friends in Africa.

The retrenchment in Moscow had an immediate effect on some African nations, especially on those authoritarian leaders such as Colonel Mengistu Haile Mariam of Ethiopia, who depended on Soviet assistance and protection to stay in power indefinitely. Soon leaders in other client states such as Angola, Congo, Mozambique, and Somalia, among many others, realized that without the overgenerous economic and military assistance from the USSR, their regimes would not survive.

Another important development that arose as a result of the weakening of the USSR was that the United States was now the only unchallenged superpower in the world. The Africans, or rather the African leaders, took notice of the Soviet situation and started to change their foreign policies to conform with the new international order. In an emerging unipolar world, the African nations had to move away from their outdated notion embedded in the so-called nonaligned approach to foreign policy.

The Non-Aligned Movement began in the former European colonies in Africa and Asia because of the terrible impact the Cold War rivalries had on those countries. Some African and Asian countries decided to establish an independent international movement to help them resist being drawn into siding with either the Western nations or the Eastern Bloc. The Non-Aligned Movement had its origins in India's long colonization experience and then the independent nonviolent struggle led by M. K. Gandhi. The colonial experience left India and many other colonies determined to avoid alliances such as NATO and the Warsaw Pact. The principle of nonalignment was the total preservation of freedom of international action through the refusal to align with any bloc or to join any alliance.

In theory, at least, the majority of African nations professed to being neutral in their dealings with the East or West. However, the truth was much more complicated. Some African countries secretly collaborated with one side or the other, depending on what was vital to their national interests at a particular time, or just to play one against the other.

When it came to the United States' dealings with the Africans, especially in the early decades of independence, Washington should have been much more mature in its handling of the relations with the young and inexperienced African nations, for the simple reason that it knew better and had the upper hand in the relationship. It is arguable that the United States had the most experienced and seasoned specialists on African affairs. Therefore, the US State Department should have acted more pragmatically toward the African nations, regardless of the latter's ideological leanings.

US credibility in Africa suffered even more because of the United States' constant decisions to deal with some of the worst dictators in sub-Saharan Africa. Washington's reasons for doing so were that those leaders were anticommunist and pro-West. Thus, the United States assumed that capitalist leaders and allies were against the USSR. The truth is that these leaders were some of the most despicable, corrupt, undemocratic, incompetent, and in some cases outright murderous thugs. To many Africans, the United States' actions just didn't make sense. Instead of improving the plight of the suffering masses, US policies were seen as being in favor of the bad rulers who were dictators in their countries and who forced the majority of their citizens to live in abject poverty—while the leaders enjoyed ostentatious lives with huge palaces in Europe and elsewhere.

These bad African leaders often used fear of Western domination to hang on to power undemocratically and claim to be the only ones capable of protecting the national sovereignty of their countries. I have always believed that these African leaders overexploited the Cold War rivalry in order to avoid owning up to their abysmal performance and the heinous mistreatment of their hapless citizens. The United States should have known that this was going to be the outcome of the confrontation between the superpowers. As a result of this confrontation, in most of these countries, especially sub-Saharan Africa, scarce national resources were diverted to support the corrupt armies and were not spent on economic development. Intelligence agencies were beefed up and set loose on innocent citizens, with dire consequences, for example, in Idi Amin's Uganda.

Partly because of Idi Amin's murderous rule in Uganda, the United States was finally forced to take action, which to many people in Africa was long overdue. President Jimmy Carter imposed stiff economic sanctions against Uganda for Idi Amin's horrendous violations of human rights and other forms of misrule in that East African nation. Although the sanctions themselves did not work as expected, it was the right and noble course for the United States to have taken.

The problem was that the United States was, as usual, very selective in the way it handled relations with these bad African governments. This double standard played out very clearly when Ronald Reagan assumed the US presidency in the 1980s. The often troubled relationship between the United States and Africa, which dated back to the advent of African independence in the 1960s, came to a head with the arrival of President Reagan. Reagan, whom I regard as perhaps the most astute and gifted political operator in modern US presidential history, decided disastrously to cooperate with the apartheid regime in South Africa. Cooperation per se was not the problem; the problem was in how far he extended it. First of all, this major policy shift came as a total surprise to many Africans because the American leaders were supposed to know the terrible situation in South Africa at that time. And regardless of the ideological stance of any US administration, they were at least expected to sympathize with the suffering majority of blacks in that country.

President Reagan elevated the Cold War rivalry to a different level, as he saw things in black and white—either you were with the United States or against the United States. The Reagan Doctrine, pronounced quite early in his administration, a strategy orchestrated and implemented by the United States under the Reagan administration to oppose the global influence of the USSR as the Cold War was coming to an end, was the centerpiece of US foreign policy from the early 1980s until the end of the Cold War in 1991. Under the Reagan Doctrine, the United States provided overt and covert aid to right-wing guerillas and resistance movements in an effort to "roll back" Soviet-backed left-wing governments in Africa, Asia, and Latin America.[1]

The Reagan Doctrine was especially significant because it represented a substantial shift in the United States. Prior to the Reagan Doctrine, US foreign policy during the Cold War was deeply rooted in "containment." Although a similar policy of rollback had been considered on a few occasions during the Cold War, the US government, fearing an escalation of the Cold War and possible nuclear conflict, chose not to confront the Soviet Union directly. Now, with the Reagan Doctrine, those fears were set aside and the United States began to openly confront Soviet-supported governments by supporting rebel movements in the doctrine's targeted countries, such as Angola and Ethiopia.[2]

Of course the majority of African countries did not accept this new extreme foreign policy position targeting some countries in the continent and therefore continued to move away from the United States. As if that were not bad enough, the Reagan administration decided to adopt a brand-new policy aimed at the apartheid regime in South Africa. The new policy, known as Constructive Engagement, was handled at the US State Department by the assistant secretary of state for African affairs, Dr. Chester Crocker.

Dr. Crocker zealously pursued this policy in total disregard of the

---

[1]   "Reagan Doctrine, 1985," US Department of State Archive, https://2001-2009. state.gov/r/pa/ho/time/rd/17741.htm.

[2]   Ibid.

protests of the African countries and the international community in general. Constructive Engagement, at least from Washington's point of view, was supposed to bring the white South African government out of isolation and help the regime to moderate some of its extreme measures against its black opponents. Washington thought that engaging the white rulers in South Africa would make them treat the blacks fairly and therefore allow the regime to permit blacks to participate in the country's theretofore segregated political arrangement. In addition, the Reagan administration hoped that its engagement with the apartheid regime would give the United States more influence in determining the future political course of South Africa—as opposed to maintaining the economic and other sanctions that had been imposed on the apartheid regime by the international community.

The South African government was more than happy with the Reagan policy, and in many ways Constructive Engagement strengthened the apartheid regime. For example, the leadership became more and more arrogant and belligerent, and repeatedly dismissed and resisted all international protests against its brutal internal security measures. The Reagan administration, on the other hand, refused even to review this policy or at least toughen the US attitude toward the apartheid regime. Meanwhile, more and more black South Africans were dying violently at the hands of the South African security forces, and many more were being systematically removed from their ancestral homes and resettled far away in the Bantustan states created by the apartheid government to accommodate blacks from different parts of South Africa. The Bantustans were created as mini sovereign tribal states meant for blacks and governed by blacks—but under the overall supervision of the South African government. This was really part of the legal segregation of the races under apartheid.

With the Constructive Engagement policy, the Reagan administration completely weakened the international sanctions placed against the South African regime. The United States used its veto power at the United Nations to block stronger measures proposed against the regime by the Security Council. This US stand continued to enrage the Africans and demonstrated that the United States did not really care how black Africans felt and was unconcerned about the human rights of black South Africans. For many Africans, Constructive Engagement prolonged the life of the apartheid regime for many more years at the expense of hundreds of lives of black South Africans.

The Bush administration, to its credit, reversed the disastrous policy and began to rebuild entente cordiale with sub-Saharan Africa. This was not easy, considering the damage that had been done between the two regions. Furthermore, the Bush administration had come to power as the crisis in Ethiopia was reaching its climax. This conflict posed the first large challenge for the Bush administration regarding its new attitude toward Africa. The United States was faced with the decision of whether to ignore the civil war or to intervene by mediating a truce between the guerillas led by Meles Zenawi and the Marxist Ethiopian regime under the dictator Mengistu H. Mariam.

The decision by the Bush administration to become directly involved in the effort to end the conflict in Ethiopia was a major turning point in US-African relations and a welcome change for the sub-Saharan nations. The United States had realized that African countries could no longer be used merely as pawns in the Cold War struggle between the superpowers. This was indeed a positive development considering the fact that many African countries were at that time undergoing serious domestic conflicts and, therefore, were badly in need of intervention from a superpower such as the United States to help stabilize the situation.

The civil war in Ethiopia between the Marxist regime of Colonel Mengistu and the opposition Eritrean People's Liberation Front (EPLF) and the Ethiopian People's Revolutionary Democratic Front (EPDRF) had been raging for a long time when the United States decided to intervene. Colonel Mengistu himself fled Ethiopia on the eve of the US-sponsored peace talks in London. Some people have speculated that the Bush administration secretly helped to get him out of the way in anticipation of a peaceful transfer of power. The long civil war, plus Mengistu's repression, forced nearly a million Ethiopian refugees out of the country and caused havoc in Ethiopia.

The OAU (Organization of African Unity, now the African Union [AU]), the UN, and other organizations had all failed in their efforts to end the conflict. Therefore, the US intervention was the only real hope for the final political settlement. The United States was represented at the talks in London by the assistant secretary of state for African affairs Herman Cohen, a career State Department official who had extensive experience with the continent.

The Ethiopian regime, now under the leadership of General Tesfaye Gebre Kidan, was at its weakest point. Tesfaye was willing to turn over power to the opposition forces. As the talks progressed, it became apparent that the United States and other Western powers were only interested in the replacement of the discredited regime in Addis Ababa. As a result, the London Conference ended with the agreement that the Kidan regime be replaced with a new government composed of the opposition forces under the interim leadership of Meles Zenawi.

However, the most regrettable outcome of that conference was the agreement to break Ethiopia into two countries, with the United States agreeing to that tragic proposition. I still do not understand why the United States acceded to the creation of Eritrea, a country that by every measure is a failed state and now has become the most

9

repressive nation in sub-Saharan Africa. Hundreds of its citizens have fled the country, especially the younger generation, in large part because of the harsh compulsory military service, which demands that soldiers serve for a longer period than any other country in the world. The United States should have rejected the separatist demands of the Eritrean People's Liberation Front and maintained the national unity of Ethiopia. The partition of this ancient African nation and kingdom set a very bad precedent in sub-Saharan Africa.

As the civil war in Ethiopia was being brought to a settlement at last, under US mediation, the other major conflict on the Horn of Africa was raging unabated. The civil war in Somalia started in 1988 among rival clans. As the conflict intensified, the already weak and repressive regime of President Mohamed Siad Barre was toppled in 1991. Barre was forced to flee the country in exile, where he ultimately died. After the departure of Barre, no effective government assumed power in Somalia.

That country was effectively left to fend for itself without a central authority and soon fell under the control of warring clans and criminal gangs who were only interested in plundering that nation and using it as a safe haven for international terrorists and criminals in exchange for money and guns. Somalia had all but become another Afghanistan in a strategically critical region that is vital in the role of international shipping to the Gulf oil states and near the volatile nation of Yemen, which borders South Arabia.

The international community, especially the United States, ignored the carnage in Somalia until the conflict began to threaten the security of the neighboring countries such as Kenya and Ethiopia, and others in the wider eastern African region. With millions of hapless Somalians starving or malnourished and displaced, and millions forced into neighboring countries, the tragically inhumane events in that country had become one of the most horrendous situations in modern African history. Various NGOs (nongovernmental organizations) such as the International Committee of the Red Cross and the Red Crescent Society tried without much success to stabilize the worsening situation.

With pressure mounting for direct action by the United States, finally, on December 4, 1992, President Bush announced US involvement and support of Operation Restore Hope. This was a UN-sanctioned operation under UN Security Council Resolution 794, but under US operational command. This operation, the first of its kind, fundamentally changed the traditional role of the UN from that of peacekeeper to peace enforcer, meaning that there could be military intervention in a civic conflict without the explicit approval of the nation involved in said civil conflict. The last time the United Nations had played a similar role was in the Korean War in the 1950s.

The US involvement in Somalia was a highly commendable humanitarian action, albeit late, and was especially important because it was in an African country. This was the kind of attitude the majority of Africans wanted to see—a caring United States willing and able to intervene to save the lives of the people and stabilize Somalia, a small country with no geostrategic value to the United States. This was America's finest hour.

Although Operation Restore Hope provided a real chance of stability in Somalia, unfortunately, as we all saw, the good mission did not go smoothly because the warring clan factions were not interested in a stable and peaceful Somalia. Restoring order in that nation would have meant taking away from the warring clans their very means of survival, such as guns, territorial control, and other illicit sources of income. Therefore, those clans were not about to let the UN's mission there succeed, regardless of the amount of destruction Somalia suffered.

Would the results have been different if the US intervention had not been strictly limited to feeding the starving and stabilizing the country, and then transferring the entire operation quickly to the UN (an organization that was clearly not in a position to handle the enormous Somalian situation on its own)? The end of the UN's humanitarian intervention in Somalia in March 1994 also ended US involvement in that country. The withdrawal left Somalia in a terrible state of anarchy. Some peace-loving Somalis and other Africans still partly blame the United States for carelessly abandoning Somalia.[3]

The termination of US involvement in Somalia, although tragic, was understandable. All the Africans and others who still blame the United States for leaving Somalia are seeing things completely wrong. The United States intervened in Somalia in order to carry out a limited humanitarian operation. However, the conditions on the ground prevented the mission from proceeding successfully. Consequently, the United States did the right thing in getting out. In addition, the new US president at the time, Bill Clinton, had other foreign policy priorities to deal with, including ongoing conflicts elsewhere in Africa. President Clinton inherited major conflicts already raging in Rwanda, Sierra Leone, Liberia, and other countries, on top of the mess left in Mogadishu.

The conflicts in some of these nations were so horrendous in terms of human degradation that they needed urgent international intervention, just like in Somalia. The war in the small east central African nation of Rwanda was one of the worst. The magnitude of the atrocities that took place there was unimaginable. President Clinton reportedly knew what was happening in Rwanda but allegedly chose not to involve the United States in that conflict, particularly at the

---

[3]   Valerie J. Lofland, "Somalia: US Intervention and Operation Restore Hope," Air University, http://www.au.af.mil/au/awc/awcgate/navy/pmi/somalia1.pdf.

height of the war. The US policy makers felt that getting involved directly in yet another self-initiated African tragedy was just too risky, and there was no public support for a major military intervention on the African continent. The experience of the failure in Somalia frightened even those US officials who would have wanted the United States to do more to stop the war in Rwanda.

Because of this, I think it is too easy and very unfair to continue blaming the United States and other Western nations for the murderous civil war in Rwanda. That conflict had been long in the making when it finally started in the early 1990s. President Juvénal Habyarimana, who ruled Rwanda from 1973 to 1994 with his political party, the National Republican Movement for Democracy and Development, strictly favored his own ethnic group, the Hutu, and promoted so much hatred of the minority Tutsi that nothing would have stopped the genocide that took place in that country.

The origins of this level of hate in Rwanda are too complex for most people to understand. However, it is true to say that the onset of Belgian colonialism in that country elevated the level of tribal division partly because of the divide-and-rule policy championed by the European colonial masters. This policy was inherited by the Rwandese themselves after independence, with disastrous consequences.

US foreign policy on Africa at that particular point in time faced myriad challenges as various nations struggled from crisis to crisis. For example, in the West African nation of Sierra Leone, the government collapsed in the 1990s, leaving the country without an effective leadership, as in Somalia. As a result, the guerillas, calling themselves the Revolutionary United Front (RUF), started a terror campaign in that small and impoverished country. Mr. Foday Sankoh, the leader of the RUF, was a murderous thug unworthy of a place in Sierra Leone, the country he almost destroyed. Sankoh had been brought into the government of Sierra Leone, led by Tejan Kabbah, for the sake of achieving peace and national reconciliation after the terrible civil war.

Some African experts and countries have blamed President Clinton for inaction in Sierra Leone, as well and for allowing Fody Sankoh to join the Kabbah government. President Clinton did provide some support to ECOMOG, a multinational peacekeeping force, but some people still think that the amount of aid was not large enough.

The usual critics of the US policy in Africa and among the diaspora still believe the outdated notion that the United States has the power to solve Africa's numerous problems and end the continent's perpetual civil wars. This is true in some special cases, such as humanitarian emergencies; however, the American people are tired of Africa's never-ending problems. All the conflicts discussed in this chapter were homegrown, in other words, started by the Africans themselves. Therefore, it is time for these African nations and citizens to stop blaming the so-called foreign enemies for their self-inflicted catastrophes.

It is time for sub-Saharan Africans to start acting and behaving like civilized and responsible people, instead of constantly doing things that demonstrate the contrary. It is true that some African nations have come a long way from the early days of independence in the 1960s. They struggled through the chaos of being young and inexperienced nations and have continued to make some hopeful progress for their citizenry. But these are just a handful of countries in a sea of mayhem, disintegration, hopelessness, irrelevancy, backwardness, and illiteracy, with a complete lack of able and upright leadership.

For this reason, African countries cannot expect the United States to continue to come to their rescue each time there is an implosion somewhere in the continent. The United States, on the whole, has been a good partner to the African nations and has generally respected the

Africans and some of their aspirations, even with the Cold War's divisions. The only time the United States did something that was counterproductive and extremely harmful to Africa was when it enacted the policy in favor of the apartheid regime of South Africa, which we discussed earlier. But even then, that policy did not stop the United States from continuing to cooperate with other nations in the continent on critical matters vital to the welfare of African citizens.

We can blame the United States for a lot of things, but it is time for the Africans to start owning up to their problems, especially the self-inflicted ones, such as the heinous wars in Rwanda, Sierra Leone, Liberia, Somalia, and other countries. As we have seen over the decades, the United States is always ready to work with African countries on various issues vital to both sides. This is not going to change as long as Africans play their part as viable partners. The problem with Africa is that in the last thirty years or so, the continent has been a place rife with discontentment, famine, hunger, poverty, military coups, lack of democratic governance, civil wars, horrendous violations of human rights, and a lot of other problems. As a result, most African countries have been nothing but basket cases. Even with the best of intentions, US leaders have found it difficult to continue justifying to the American people the importance of cooperating with and assisting these African countries when these nations have completely failed to make the kind of progress we have seen in Asia, the Pacific Rim, the Middle East, and Latin America. As more and more African nations continue to splinter, with the latest being the Sudan, we are going to see more problems emerging in these new countries. And that will continue to pose serious challenges to US policy makers when it comes to how to handle the new problems, on top of the traditional ones we have discussed.

The United States cannot afford to continue wasting its money and other forms of assistance on countries that show a very serious lack of purpose and that lack the foresight necessary to achieve sound transformation and national progress. The ongoing conflicts in some parts of the Sudan such as Darfur, and in the newly independent South Sudan, in which the United States is already deeply involved, demonstrate this lack. The Bush administration worked very hard to bring the Second Sudanese Civil War to an end and committed billions of dollars toward that nation's reconstruction after almost forty years of destructive civil wars. The problem is that South Sudanese themselves are seriously divided. This does not bode well for the future of that country.

The United States, especially the intelligence community, should continue to monitor the situation in South Sudan very closely. President Bush and former secretary of state Colin Powell deserve to be highly commended for the seriousness with which they dealt with the Sudanese conflict. It was one of President Bush's good deeds in Africa. Hopefully he will be remembered for it.

2

Helping Africa to Strengthen Its Political and Governing Institutions

The United States and other Western democracies have always had a love–hate relationship with Africa because the Western nations tend to measure and compare the standards of African democratic and civic institutions against their own, and then judge these African institutions harshly when they fail to live up to these unrealistically high standards. Africans, as is the case with people of all other developing countries, are still trying, with extreme difficulty, to develop democratic institutions that will suit their unique societies and peoples. This is most certainly not to excuse the enormous failures of democracy in Africa, but it is just the reality.

What the United States, in particular, should do is to continue working with these countries and helping them to grow and strengthen their democratic systems. This is the only way forward, as ostracizing and bullying these poor nations will get them nowhere. As we saw in the previous chapter, of course the USA must demand something in return for the help it provides. It is in the best interest of African countries for the United States to do so. Otherwise, the usual bad practices will just continue unabated. The African countries have not performed well in almost all major indexes that point to upward development and general national progress. The continent, in particular the sub-Sahara, measures very poorly in general macroeconomic advancement, and poorly in almost all areas of social development, such as health care, education, food sufficiency, housing, and employment, among many others.

Africa's failures are by no means the failures of the African people. They are really the terrible failures of the national institutions controlled by bad leaders. Ordinary Africans are smart, enterprising, ambitious, thoughtful, hardworking, intelligent, and hopeful— just like successful people in the United States, Europe, Asia, and elsewhere. What these Africans want most, but have always lacked, is good leadership, manageable or fair democracy, political stability, personal security, and respect for their human rights and economic freedom. This is surely not too much to ask.

This is where America's help is badly needed. The United States and African countries should agree to start an annual summit conference where the leaders sit down together to discuss US-African relations. Talk about the numerous problems African countries are facing and how to tackle them one by one is vital. African leaders meet with the Chinese leadership annually to discuss Chinese-African relations. Why not have a similar summit with the single most important country in the world—frankly, the nation with the kind of values Africans aspire to have.

The United States has many resources that it can deploy in different countries, resources especially needed in sub-Saharan Africa. Of course the countries of sub-Saharan Africa must be honestly willing and able to play their part seriously. The American people are some of the most generous on the face of the earth. I have no doubt whatsoever that they want to see Africa as prosperous as the United States, and continuing to make progress.

The Africans, on their part, should seriously learn from the Asians, the Europeans, and the people of other newly emerging successful nations who have enormously benefited from the United States' generosity and goodwill—especially in the twentieth century. In Europe, the Marshall Plan rehabilitated the continent after World War II. In Japan, the United States undertook to protect and rebuild the island nation. The United States also helped the Republic of Korea get to where it is today—one of the most powerful economies in the world. Now, the most important point here is that these nations truly benefited from and were heavily assisted by the involvement of the United States. However, it was also their efforts, determination, seriousness, vision, high hopes, and hard work that made it possible.

If Africans want the United States to make a long-term commitment in their countries, then they must be prepared to abandon their failed ways of doing business and their outdated practices. For example, Africans must begin to move away from nepotism and tribal ways of thinking. These practices are as old as Africa itself, but clearly they have no place in modern African society. Africans will never convince the American people that they are seriously committed to the principles of humanitarian respect and democracy unless they start treating each other fairly and with respect, regardless of their ethnic or tribal differences. The American people want to see a peaceful African continent with all the nations there being well governed and forward-looking, pursuing market-oriented economic methods, and striving very hard to establish multiparty or plural democratic traditions, all while respecting the rule of law.

Some usual critics of this way of reasoning are going to insist that this is too much to demand from these poor nations, saying that it also smacks of Western imperial ideas, which Africa is not yet ready for. I beg to differ. This is really not too much to ask. After all, the Indians have accomplished it; the Chinese are slowly making strides toward the same goals; the central and east Europeans have done it; and the Latin Americans have become generally successful countries. Therefore, why not the Africans? What is so unique about Africans that makes them less capable of organizing themselves ably and doing what is right in their respective nations?

The majority of African people are now educated, with a large number of them firmly in the middle-class ranks, and with millions of others doing very well in the private business sector. Interestingly, the majority of these educated Africans prefer and admire Western values, especially the way of life in the United States. Amicable cooperation with the United States is what most of African citizens really want. They like the kind of freedom the Americans enjoy; they like free market enterprise; they like the freedom of the press, and also they like the United States' popular culture and fashion (e.g., music, cinema, clothes).

This new generation of Africans doesn't carry the baggage of the older generations, who still tend to view the West with suspicion and fear because of their colonial experiences. Frankly, they have reasons to be afraid. Luckily, the United States has no colonial history in Africa. It warmly welcomed the final independence of African countries from their European colonial masters. This is a very good foundation to build upon, and some African leaders have been doing just that—although without a lot of success. There is definitely more work to be done on both sides—with perhaps a lot more on the African side.

The countries in Africa must start by clearly setting out their major priorities and properly sorting out what they can accomplish on their own and where they critically need help from the United States. For starters, African countries must eliminate completely the role of the military in their national political discourse. This is a prerequisite for everything, because constant military intervention in politics has been a disaster for the Africans and is what has kept a number of African nations from moving forward. The sub-Saharan countries must also strive to eliminate corruption, which is pervasive in the region, and establish clear transparency in the way their governments function, from the local level to the national level. If done well, this could increase the level of confidence their American friends have that the African countries are at last beginning to clean house and thus becoming worthy and deserving of America's goodwill and, most importantly, of serious economic, political, and security assistance from the United States to achieve both short- and long-term goals.

The United States is not going to come and undertake the task of nation building in Africa. However, the United States can help the African people in several critical areas. For example, African nations could use the United States' expertise and resources to rebuild and strengthen important governmental and other national institutions that are critical for fostering a strong democracy—these being the judiciary, bureaucracy (civil service), parliamentary systems, political parties, and an independent media.

Most people, friends and foes alike, would agree that in the majority of African countries, the rule of law just does not exist. What you find instead is the rule of the jungle. Even where there is some kind of judicial practice, it is often administered at the whim of those in power. This has not only led to grievous violations of human rights but also frightened many foreign investors from bringing their capital and other investments to sub-Saharan Africa. No investor wants to go to any country where there is no rule of law to protect private investments. The United States could assist greatly in this regard.

The USA can also help a great deal to turn very weak bureaucratic systems in the continent into properly functioning and efficient systems. No country can work or function effectively without a well-trained bureaucratic system. Africa, as a whole, is in serious need of well-educated and highly motivated bureaucrats for the region's very survival! African countries are lagging behind other developing nations, partly because of the weaknesses of the administrative standards in the various AU countries. It may come as a surprise to many people in other parts of the world that the majority of African countries have just a few well-trained professionals in important positions such as accountants, financial analysts, budget experts, public administration specialists, trained managers, engineers, and even lower-level technicians critical to the smooth administration of any viable nation. The African nations have never made serious investments in the development of their human resources, unlike the nations of Asia. Here again, the United States can be of assistance.

To train a large number of people takes time and a lot of capital, the latter of which African countries just don't have. There are many excellent private organizations in the United States, especially the think tanks, which are always willing and able to undertake the enormous task of training and reorganizing the antiquated administrative structures in Africa that, in most cases, were set up by the European colonial powers. The systems are now seriously outdated and often dysfunctional. And to make matters worse, African countries have experienced population explosions on top of all their other problems. This, therefore, means that many more people badly need good governmental services in their respective countries—something that can only be attained if these administrative structures are thoroughly reformed and placed in capable hands.

Anybody who follows or is an observer of political developments in Africa is probably aware that legislative systems (parliament), like the judicial systems are weaker in Sub-Saharan Africa than anywhere else in the world. Parliament is a major institution in many democratic systems, yet in Africa, the national legislatures are nothing but a laughable joke. In order to strengthen democratic rule, African countries must reform their political systems so that parliament becomes the heart and soul of their governments. In addition, parliaments can and should act as the most powerful check on the actions of the often corrupt and abusive governments.

African nations do not have experience with a constitutional parliamentary system of government. Therefore, these countries need help from an experienced democratic nation, such as the United States, to enable them to transform their political systems in ways that will make them work more efficiently for the overall betterment of the citizens of Africa.

As we know all too well, having a strong parliamentary system without equally strong and democratic political parties is not going to bring stability or the kind of success Africa is desperately seeking. The sub-Saharan countries have not developed or nurtured credible, well-organized political parties since they became independent. What these countries have are really parties in name only. And in country after country, the politicians have created political parties that they own and tightly control. These parties, run undemocratically, are usually headed by the self-appointed life presidents. The political parties, therefore, are used as tools or mechanisms for tribal or ethnic domination, corrupt practices, patronage, and total domination of their respective countries. As a result, the rulers become completely alienated from the rest of the citizenry, and the discontent ultimately turns into violence and civil disorder.

Therefore, seriously reforming Africa's governing structures must include a change in the way the political parties are organized and run. Again, this is an area where the United States has a great deal of expertise. The United States can truly help Africans to properly modernize and reform their political parties and, more importantly, help to train the political cadres on how to run efficient, effective, and democratic political party systems for a resurgent, energetic, mobile, young, and forward-looking sub-Saharan Africa.

It is critical that Africans modernize and thoroughly improve their governing systems. Without doing so, the continent's future will forever be doomed! The last fifty years have been a total waste for the citizens of Africa. Let the continent, especially sub-Sahara, not waste the next fifty years of the twenty-first century. The leaders in Africa must stop kidding themselves. Sub-Sahara urgently needs a huge amount of help from the United States in the vital areas we have discussed, and perhaps much, much more.

Helping Africa to build strong and viable national institutions is just one aspect that must be undertaken. However, African countries also need to encourage and nurture the culture of a free press and allow their citizens to freely organize civic groups and, from time to time, stand up to protest against their governments without being mistreated or killed. These and other rights are taken for granted in the United States, and I strongly believe that the United States is a better place because of these constitutional rights. The people of Africa want these same rights.

Africans want their countries to start functioning like all other successful nations in the world. They want law and order, excellent public services, vibrant and well-managed economies, superb infrastructure, clean air, beautiful cities, good schools, adequate health care, proper housing, clean water, enough food provisions, and high-quality affordable goods. They also want freedom to freely practice their religions, along with, of course, good and democratically run governments.

The United States and other developed nations have been reluctant to commit or invest significantly in Africa because, deep down, they believe that Africa is a hopeless case. Therefore, they think it will be a waste of their precious resources to intervene. I think that the United

States, and the West in general, is probably right. But my contention is that the status quo in Africa is even more dangerous. The United States must not write off Africa. Instead, it must be involved in all the efforts to renew and rebuild Africa. Yes, the relationship has been less than amicable for the last fifty or so years, but now is an opportunity for the United States to demonstrate to the people of Africa that it really cares and that it is willing and ready to invest whatever it takes to give genuine hope to sub-Saharan Africa.

My experience tells me that a lot of Americans still care a great deal about the African situation, as demonstrated by their responses to natural and other disasters on the continent. However, I think Americans are at a loss when it comes to what to do or how to meaningfully help Africa. I am not one of those people who think that the US assistance should mostly be in the form of money and consumer goods. I, rather, believe that aid to sub-Saharan Africa must mainly be in the form of man power in crucial areas such as governance, farming, building construction, road and bridge construction, water management, urban development, and the provision of heavy equipment and other tools that African nations severely lack. The best way to help sub-Saharan countries is to enable them to become self-sufficient. That, I am certain, will restore their confidence, self-worth, and honor.

This is the moment for American leaders to be forthright with the despotic African leaders, instead of offering the usual meaningless diplomatic platitudes, while Africa continues to burn and decay. Sub-Saharan Africa has some of the most fertile soil in the world, with hundreds of rivers, lakes, rich deserts, and many, many other useful resources—which should make the continent one of the wealthiest places on earth. And yet sub-Sahara remains the poorest place imaginable. A large number of people in the region suffer from famine, malnutrition, and poor health, and still live in deplorable and inhuman conditions. This situation is totally unacceptable in our modern world. The African people, with assistance of the United States, could turn things around. They are just waiting for the opportunity and proper guidance—something that they do not get from their leaders.

President Bush took the struggle for democracy to the Middle East, and that set the ball rolling for political freedom. Now we are seeing the results of that strategically important initiative. The people of the Middle East and the northern part of Africa have risen up to demand more democratic governmental systems and generally more freedom for themselves and future generations. It is time for a US president to do the same thing with Africa.

This is not a call for another war, but a direct initiative by a US president to save Africa, especially sub-Sahara. Intervening in sub-Sahara with good ideas and intentions, and with the necessary tools to rebuild those poverty-stricken nations from the bottom up, not only will be welcomed by the masses in Africa but will also, most importantly, cement the critical relationship between the two partners for centuries to come. This relationship, I believe, is vital to the stability of the world. Surely, the United States and Africa should be natural allies just like the United States and European nations are allies. The people of African descent have been part of the United States since the time of the founding of this Great Republic. This, in my view, makes the relationship between Africa and the United States very special indeed.

However, partly because of the reasons we have discussed and some other, unknown facts, American leaders have always tended to de-emphasize the relationship with Africa in favor of the relationship with Europe and Asia. Of course Asia is a very wealthy region and Asia's economies have expanded in such a way that it is hard for the United States to ignore. Nevertheless, sub-Saharan Africa also has a lot to offer to the United States, from highly valued natural resources (minerals and oil) to other greater investment opportunities for American companies. Therefore, constantly viewing sub-Sahara as a charity case must come to an end. Let us teach Africans how to catch the fish and stop the old-fashioned culture of aid and donations with perennial financial bailouts.

All the forty-eight or so sub-Saharan countries are at different stages and levels of economic development. The majority are still extremely poor, with the average per capita income being less than US$500. Only the Republic of South Africa is ranked at the middle level of economic development, with just a handful of others somewhere near the middle of the economic ladder. However, in the past few years, there has been some good news coming out of the African continent. Even the very poorest countries have started to make some minor but necessary reforms to their economies. This step, though very small and still fraught with all sorts of problems, must be encouraged and backed by the United States. These countries have a long way to go, but a move in the right direction, however small, is always welcome. A bit of encouragement at this pivotal time could continue that motion in the direction of progress.

The causes for Africa's puzzling underdevelopment are numerous and extremely complex, and perhaps a topic for another book. But suffice it to say here that the people of Africa are determined, now more than ever, to pull themselves up from the depths of despair and hopelessness. And the United States must be there to help them. If this happens, then in the end, the United States will be the winner, because Africans will always attribute their economic emancipation and democratic liberation to what is still the greatest nation on the face of the earth.

For those countries in Africa still clinging to the past and not prepared to give the United States a chance, they will be condemned by history and permanently relegated to that infamous group known as the Least Developed Countries (LDCs). As a result, almost all of their educated class will continue to leave for greener pastures, especially to Europe and North America. A considerable number of African intellectuals have been leaving the continent for a number of years now because they don't see a light at the end of the tunnel. And this sad phenomenon has compounded Africa's problem, as nation after nation has been left in the hands of largely ill-educated rulers and bureaucrats (civil servants). Just imagine the USA being run by illiterates!

The African people are desperate and seriously yearning for their currently abysmal economic, political, and social situation to change and improve. And who can blame them for feeling that way? These people have not experienced the good life for the last forty or more years. Yet their counterparts in Asia, South America, and even most of the former USSR countries are enjoying unprecedented economic prosperity and democratic freedom. Without any doubt, these successes are due, in large measure, to those peoples' willingness to embrace, and most crucially accept, unswervingly, the political, military, and economic guidance and assistance of the United States.

This, of course, does not mean that these Asian, South American, and other successful nations are lackeys or stooges of the United States. To the contrary, these countries know what is in their national interests and are willing to do everything within their power to get what they want—and that is all that matters.

3

Economic Relations

From the advent of political independence in Africa in the 1960s, trade and other relations between the United States and Africa have never been easy. The warm US enthusiasm that greeted Africa's independence soon gave way to serious doubts, and other problems that developed under the Cold War. Sub-Saharan Africa, as already mentioned in the previous chapter, figured very low to US foreign-policy makers on virtually every issue.

However, to be fair to the United States, sub-Sahara has never been a major trade or economic power compared to the Asian region. The reasons are not hard to point out. When the colonial European countries took over Africa and carved it up into smaller nations, they apparently did not have in mind the idea or plan to develop these colonies into successful industrial economies. What the colonial powers did was to set up a system whereby sub-Sahara was to be used only as the primary marketing grounds for manufactured consumer goods and services from Europe. The colonists were made to rely on the European products, whether they liked them or not, and Africa became an important source of raw materials for the industries in Europe.

This practice is one of the critical reasons why sub-Saharan Africa is as poor as it is today. In the colonial era, all the countries in Africa traded almost exclusively with the European powers that colonized them. For example, the British colonies, such as Uganda, Kenya, Ghana, and Nigeria, traded mostly with Britain. The same economic system was practiced in the French, Portuguese, and Spanish colonies in Africa. This trading system obviously gave the Europeans an enormous advantage and tremendous economic success.

As a result, the European colonizers made sure that Africa, especially sub-Sahara, remained the producers of just a few cash crops, such as coffee, cotton, tobacco, and tea, and the producers of minerals and other commodities for export. Uganda has continued to be an exporter of mainly agricultural commodities such as coffee, tobacco, tea, and cotton, and minerals like copper, since it gained independence in 1962. Uganda never significantly diversified its economy after colonialism ended, almost fifty years ago.

This is the case in virtually all sub-Saharan countries—the economic systems left behind by the colonial rulers have proven to be extremely difficult to change or reform. One would have expected, for instance, Uganda and other African countries, by now, to be producing and exporting various brands of pure first-class coffee, tea, textiles, and cigarettes, and manufacturing various types of copper-based products for domestic consumption and export. But, unfortunately, this has not happened! As a result, Uganda is still a minor player in global economic and trade affairs. The fact is that countries don't get rich by just selling a few cash crops—they get rich when they start to produce, on a massive scale, lots of globally marketable goods. Sub-Saharan Africa is still far behind in this regard.

And the situation is not likely to change, so long as the status quo reigns with regard to these countries' poor political leadership and bad governance remain. Africa can do better than this with the right leadership and sound free market policies. One seriously wonders how the Asian and South American nations have made major strides in developing their economies when some of these countries were much poorer than some sub-Saharan countries in the early 1960s. The major difference was, and still is, the caliber of political leadership. In Asia, South America, and other emerging nations, the leaders, although somewhat corrupt and autocratic, nevertheless were, and still are, committed to undertaking the painful but necessary economic reforms and doing whatever is possible to grow their economies. As a result, these nations have all but conquered extreme poverty and are now major players on the world economic stage.

Look at the progress of the countries that belong to BRICS. These countries, namely, Brazil, India, China, and Russia, and now, for unknown reasons, the Republic of South Africa, are economically growing at astonishing rates, compared to all other nations, especially the OECD (Organisation for Economic Co-operation and Development) member countries. The BRICS countries have gone through painful reforms, and with good reasons have adopted market-oriented economic systems just like the US economic method. And, of course, all of them are major trading partners of the United States. This proves the point that economic freedom and crucial close collaboration with the United States is enormously vital for any country, especially those in the least developed parts of the world such as Africa.

The economic achievements of these BRICS nations have been spectacular, especially when we consider the fact that it took them just a few decades to achieve what has taken other countries centuries to accomplish. The people of these places are not superhumans. The one thing they all possess is the high drive to succeed; their single-minded determination has been relentless.

Could this also happen in the larger sub-Saharan Africa in our lifetime? I strongly believe and hope so. With the help of the United States, sub-Sahara can turn things around. The United States has a gigantic consumer market, which can be very beneficial to sub-Saharan nations, but only to those countries with the potential for economic growth and fairly good political leadership. The United States has already taken the first major step to seriously improve economic relations with sub-Saharan countries, for the very first time in the continent's postcolonial history.

Since the early part of the last decade (2000), the US trade and investment relationship with sub-Sahara has greatly improved, with the efforts mainly coming from the US side—thanks to the determination of some American leaders who fortunately still care about Africa in general. All these encouraging developments, of course, would have been impossible without the complete end of apartheid rule in the old South Africa. The acrimonious atmosphere between the two regions started to abate after the minority regime in South Africa agreed to democratically turn over political power to the black majority in that country.

As a result, in 1993, the US Congress began lifting all antiapartheid restrictions imposed on South Africa over the course of several years, and in 1994 Congress directed the US government to come up with a comprehensive trade and development policy for the countries of sub-Saharan Africa. Consequently, in May 2000, Congress approved the African Growth and Opportunity Act (AGOA). The main intention of Congress in approving the AGOA was to grant preferential treatment to selected imports from a few eligible nations that truly demonstrated ability and were seriously trying to move toward market-oriented economic systems—nations that also had a respect for the rule of law and that respected the human rights of their workers.[4]

---

[4] Danielle Langton, "US Trade and Investment Relationship with Sub-Saharan Africa: The African Growth and Opportunity Act and Beyond," CRS Report for Congress, updated October 28, 2008, https://digital.library.unt.edu/ark:/67531/metadc463418/m1/1/high_res_d/RL31772_2008Oct28.pdf.

This was no small victory for the Africans. The people who know a little bit about the workings of the US political system know that this was a major step forward in postindependence African-US economic relations. It took a lot of lobbying and campaigning on the part of those people in the United States who are genuinely still interested in furthering relations with Africa, particularly sub-Sahara.

Since AGOA was enacted in 2005, has trade significantly improved between the two regions? Not very much—because before this law, US trade with and investment in sub-Saharan Africa comprised only 1–2 percent of the US volume for the entire world, although the figures available show that total trade, that is, exports plus imports with sub-Sahara, increased by approximately 32 percent from 2009 to 2010.[5]

However, this is still extremely insignificant in comparison to the total US trade with other nations or regions of the world. For example, for the US trade with Canada and Mexico alone is bigger than that with the whole of sub-Saharan Africa (SSA). In addition, US-SSA trade is only concentrated in a few areas, and mostly on commodities such as minerals, oil, agricultural products, and textiles. The truth is that sub-Sahara has much less to offer to the consumers in the United States than, say, China and India. That is why trade between the two regions is lop-sided in favor of the United States, because the United States produces more industrial goods and offers more top services (technical, financial, etc.) than the Africans.

Therefore, this situation is not likely to change in the foreseeable future, until the trading partners in sub-Sahara do what the Asian nations have done, which is to drastically transform their economies and focus more on manufacturing high-value goods for export. The Asians have done this so well that today, their economies are

---

[5] Ibid.

dependent on exports for the huge growth we have seen in that region in the last few decades.

This, therefore, is another area that sub-Sahara needs assistance in. The US government and private companies must go to these countries and try to help them to develop better ways of managing their economies. Africa deserves this from the United States. US companies must stop being afraid of sub-Saharan Africa because of the political instability or lack of democracy in the region. I strongly believe that a sizable presence of the United States' major corporations in sub-Sahara would most certainly cause African leaders to establish and maintain stability, instill confidence, and allow for the much needed free market economic experience that the Africans still badly lack. The American companies are, perhaps, not aware that some sub-Saharan countries possess a sufficient labor force and that, more importantly, labor is still very cheap.

US corporations can set up their manufacturing operations in sub-Sahara to produce consumer goods of all types cheaply for the US market, just like they are doing in China, India, Brazil, Vietnam, and elsewhere in emerging nations. We must, however, also keep in mind that Africa itself is becoming a giant consumer market, which I strongly wish US companies would take advantage of. The more US companies do business with Africa, the better for both regions. I have always wondered why the titans of US corporations have miserably failed to penetrate the African market.

Right from the advent of independence in the 1960s, US businesses have been minor players in Africa. Instead, Africa economies have been heavily dominated by European businesses and, more recently, by the Asian giants Japan and China. And there no major efforts are being made by the United States to change this situation. Some of us want the situation to change in favor of American companies. I discussed this issue in my blog (*Lazarus' Opinion*, lazarusopinion.

blogspot.com[6]) some time back, in a post related to one of the most important US manufacturing industries: the auto industry. The following reflects my opinion regarding US motor vehicles and the African market:

US Automakers Still Ignoring Africa

The story of the Big Three US automakers, Daimler Chrysler, Ford, and GMC, is now well known to all of us. The truth is that all of them are seriously struggling, with GMC and Chrysler suffering the most. These two once giant corporations are still in existence only because the US government rightly bailed them out by partially nationalizing them. GMC was once the envy of the world. We all mistakenly thought that these companies were being managed by the best and brightest people in America.

The US companies are well known for their aggressive competition on the global scale. They go after every viable market in the world. In the past few decades, the focus was on the newly emerging nations or newly industrialized countries in South Asia, South America, Central Asia, the Middle East, and to some extent Africa. However, in all these markets, the US automakers have either very limited presence or total absence! Take Africa, for example: US automakers have never established a foothold in that vast continent.

---

[6]   Note that all blog posts have been edited to bring punctuation, capitalization, and other minor issues in line with the style prevalent throughout *Cordial Relations between Africa and the United States in the Twenty-First Century.*

Growing up in Uganda (East Africa) in the 1960s, I was surrounded only by European vehicles. Interestingly, this was the case in almost all African countries. Toward the end of the 1960s, Japanese vehicles started to appear on the African market, but these were still far outnumbered by European automobiles. Completely absent from these markets were, as usual, the US automakers. I do not know what the leaders of Chrysler, Ford, and GMC were thinking, but the truth is that it was shortsightedness and bad judgment in the 1960s, as it is now, to continue ignoring the African market.

Ask the Japanese and European automakers about Africa. I strongly believe that all of them would say that their involvement in Africa over the decades has been extremely beneficial to their respective companies. The US automakers once dominated the US market. However, that is no longer the case. Foreign vehicles are now competing very well on the American market—actually better than most US brands. Therefore, the American automakers should look elsewhere for new markets. I think Africa is one such market.[7]

It is important to note that this post was written long before the US auto industry made a major turnaround, which happened in the last two years or so. These three giants have cleaned up their acts

---

[7] *Lazarus' Opinion*, January 12, 2012, http://lazarusopinion.blogspot.com/2010/01/us-automakers-still-ignoring-africa.html.

and are making very good vehicles for the US market and global markets. GMC is once again the number one automaker in the world, with Ford and Chrysler not far behind. This is definitely very good news. Therefore, I hope these companies will take my advice and start looking positively at the African market.

After writing about my opinion on the US auto industry, I discussed Walmart's global strategies, especially its lack of interest in the African market. I wrote to the Walmart chairman and posted the letter on my blog, as follows:

Walmart Should Invest in Africa

Dear Mr. Chairman:

First of all, congratulations for the success of your company. My purpose in writing this letter to you is to express what I think about the globalization of Walmart, especially concerning your lack of expansion in the emerging markets in Africa.

To the best of my knowledge, Walmart has extended its businesses to South America, Europe, Asia, and other parts of the world, but not Africa. I am not suggesting that you move into the continent overnight. What I think is wise for Walmart to do is to start looking at selected markets in Africa and enter into those markets before other companies do. I have looked at your remarkable success in Mexico, an economy comparable to that of a lot of African countries.

For example, Nigeria alone has about 150 million citizens, who want all types of consumer products and have the resources for buying them. Right now, the only major stores that exist in some African countries are those from South Africa. However, these stores are not like Walmart. They are much smaller and do not carry the kind of products that Walmart brings to its customers.

Mr. Chairman, the nations of Africa are getting their economies in good shape, and that means the rise in the standards of living of hundreds of millions of real consumers. I am sure that those African consumers are going to demand the kind of products and services your company offers. Take the opportunity—do not rely on what you read about Africa in the media. There are major American companies such as Coca-Cola and a few others already operating in Africa, very successfully for years. Why can't Walmart join these companies and establish itself in what is going to be the continent of opportunities?

I am only doing this because I strongly believe that the presence of Walmart in Africa will be beneficial to the company, but I also help to strengthen and solidify the free enterprise culture in the continent. Africans are free market oriented by nature, but a major company like Walmart, which is a symbol of success and responsibility, would really make a huge difference in that continent.[8]

Interestingly, at the time I was putting together *Cordial Relations between Africa and the United States in the Twenty-First Century:*

---

[8] "Walmart Should Invest in Africa," *Lazarus' Opinion*, February 10, 2010, http://lazarusopinion.blogspot.com/2010/02/walmart-should-invest-in-africa.html.

How the United States Can Help to Transform the Continent, Walmart had just started a small but positive involvement in sub-Sahara—in the country of South Africa. This is exactly the kind of US corporate investment sub-Sahara badly needs. Now, I hope more major American business entities will follow suit and establish their presence in arguably the fastest-growing market today.

Since this posting, which was based partly on the information I received directly from Walmart Company—the latest information now indicates that the Company's investments in Africa is slowly growing and that is a very hopeful achievement.

The nations of sub-Sahara are struggling to get out of the economic doldrums they have been in for the last forty or so years. However, these countries are not going to make it on their own—mainly because they lack capital, trained human resources, a literate populace, and good governance. Therefore, the salvation for these countries lies to a great extent with the USA. The United States must help sub-Saharan nations solve these teething problems, because these problems are hindering the smooth flow of direct foreign investments to the region, with dire consequences for the poor people of sub-Sahara.

In addition to the problems mentioned above, sub-Saharan countries are still consumed by problems such as unreliable power supply, corruption, extremely poor infrastructure, and of course bureaucratic red tape. These are monumental problems and the major impediment to the continent's economic advancement. It will take time for sub-Sahara to successfully convert or adapt to the East Asian model of export-led manufacturing, or even service-led growth. But that is the only way to sustain prosperity. The Asian countries have employed this model so well that now some of them have almost caught up to the developed OECD countries—and within the shortest period in economic history.

That said, the most important factor to keep in mind here is that without the huge open US market, these Asian tigers would not have achieved the kind of economic success we have witnessed in these regions in the past few decades. Now I believe it is time for sub-Saharan Africa to receive this benefit. African countries are fully aware that their present predicaments are simply untenable. Therefore, it is incumbent upon them to step up to the plate and start to do what is right for their respective citizens. The United States is not going to do everything for them, and it shouldn't have to. The African countries must meet he United States halfway with credible ideas and plans for how to emancipate themselves economically.

The United States has already set the ball rolling in the enactment of AGOA and the adoption of other positive policy measures. The AGOA is a very powerful tool in the hands of the sub-Saharan countries, which must not allow this once-in-a-lifetime opportunity to pass without concrete achievements for the African region. It will be a terrible thing if the Africans fail to take advantage of this chance to once and for all transform the economic fortunes of Africa in the early part of this century.

This is a brand-new opportunity for Africa. The Cold War is over, and there is a new and much better attitude in the United States toward Africa. The American business community currently views Africa a bit more favorably than in the past. This is critical, because it is the business community the Africans need most. Africa must convince US businesses that the region is both wide open for serious business and very safe for their capital investments.

The last fifty years were a total waste in terms of cooperation between Africa and the United States. Let this century be different. We cannot in good conscience continue to allow sub-Sahara to remain the poorest and least developed subregion in the world. It is bad for the international community; it is bad for stability and the world order; and most importantly it is an unnecessary burden on developed Western democracies.

Aid and developmental assistance from multilateral institutions such as the World Bank, the International Monetary Fund, and the United Nations Development Program, and from developed countries, has been a total failure. Sadly, this aid and assistance has helped to keep the Africans from working hard and struggling to be self-reliant like the Asians. For many years, as long as Africans got some handouts from the West and had their national budgets covered by the same Western nations, they had nothing to worry about.

Nevertheless, it is very encouraging to see that some African countries have finally realized that depending too much on foreign aid has been a disaster. Therefore, they are now aggressively attempting to reform, correct, and diversify their economies. This entails a serious focus on international trade to improve economic growth and also encourage and spur domestic consumption. This is a very hopeful sign, and very good for the long-term future of AGOA.

The United States and its partners in Africa can work together amicably to deal with other outstanding issues concerning AGOA, such as the expansion of the eligible countries beyond Nigeria, South Africa, Angola, the Republic of Congo, Lesotho, Kenya, Cameroon, and Mauritius. In addition, sub-Saharan countries should diversify AGOA exports away from mainly primary commodities such as oil, minerals, and agricultural goods, and manufacture high-value consumer goods for the US market.

The US government is providing technical assistance and trade capacity support to AGOA beneficiary countries. This effort must be ongoing until such a time that African nations are able to stand on their own. The US Congress and US citizens clearly understand this. Presidents Clinton and Bush understood that Africa's continued progress depended in large part on America's assistance. That is why the two presidents were instrumental in laying the groundwork that eventually led to the final enactment of AGOA. President Clinton helped to change the US attitude toward Africa, especially after the bloody Cold War and the bitter disagreement over the handling of the apartheid regime in South Africa.

After the end of apartheid rule in South Africa, President Clinton, in 1994, proposed US$600,000,000 in aid and investment for that country—perhaps the largest amount of US assistance in sub-Saharan Africa. And in 1997, he proposed the Partnership for Economic Growth and Opportunity in Africa, which offered different levels of economic benefits to the countries in sub-Saharan Africa, depending on those nations' economic reform measures.

These initiatives were extremely important, especially coming from the United States. Africans were not used to seeing such positive policy proposals meant to benefit their region and respective countries. The people of Africa had always been led to believe that the United States and other Western democracies had a secret agenda of undermining Africa and keeping it the poorest continent. But President Clinton's actions proved that there was nothing of the sort, in the United States at least.

On the other hand, President Bush, who came to office without a deep understanding of the African situation, ended up surprising many traditional skeptics by doing even more for the Africans than almost all other US presidents had in recent times. His initiative on HIV/AIDS assistance to sub-Sahara came at a very opportune moment, considering that thousands of African men, women, and children were dying of this killer disease. There is more about this in another chapter.

The most important thing is that the Bush administration did not let the momentum of trade and investments in sub-Sahara begun in the Clinton era die down, as was the usual practice. Bush continued to work with Congress and other interested parties until AGOA was enacted into law in May of 2000. It is still too early to rate the overall success of AGOA, but what we are sure of is that the benefits of AGOA to the African region will be slow in materializing. However, in the long term, sub-Saharan Africa will be the winner.

4

Strategic Relations—United States Africa Command

The second most important development, apart from the trading cooperation act (AGOA), in US-African relations in the last fifty years was the creation of the United States Africa Command—a critical unified regional military establishment meant specifically for the maintenance of peace and security in the Africa region. The establishment of AFRICOM in February of 2007 by President Bush was definitely long overdue, considering the rising security challenges in the region and the growing importance of African oil to the United States.

AFRICOM is currently headquartered at Kelley Barracks, Stuttgart, Germany. AFRICOM's responsibilities cover the entire African continent, except the North African country of Egypt, which is under USCENTCOM, the military command for the Middle Eastern area. In addition, Egypt is a prominent member of the Arab League, the political organization for the Arab countries in the Middle East and northern Africa.

The US administrations and Congress, right from the beginning of the independence of the African nations in the late 1950s and '60s, tended to view sub-Saharan Africa as a region with insignificant strategic value to the United States. However, now with ever-growing international terrorism, whether politically or criminally motivated, the fact is that it is posing serious threats to the United States' critical national interests throughout Africa and on the island nations associated with the continent.

For some of us who had always advocated for the establishment of the command—to demonstrate the United States' concern for Africa, just as it had done for other regions of the world, this was a very welcome move by the United States. I stated my views about the creation of the AFRICOM in my blog in November 2009, as follows:

The United States Africa Command – AFRICOM

The United States Africa Command was created in February 2007 to oversee the strategic interests of the United States in Africa and the surrounding areas—especially on the high seas bordering the African continent. In establishing the United States Africa Command, the United States did what it has already done for other vital regions of the world, such as the Pacific, the Near East, South Asia, and Europe. Actually, I think it took the United States a very long time to finally decide to set up AFRICOM.

According to the US government, AFRICOM will focus on preventing wars. In this effort, the United States intends to work with African nations and local organizations to promote regional security and crisis-response capacity in support of America's overall work in Africa. This is a very noble idea indeed.

However, the reactions in Africa to AFRICOM have been mixed at best. Some countries have welcomed it, while others have expressed the usual unfounded suspicions about US military dominance. The United States is right to establish this command. Whether we like it or not, Africa is becoming a very important continent, too important for the United States to continue to ignore. The growth of international terrorism and the constant political instability in most of the African countries are matters of great concern to the United States. Just look at the Sudan, Mauritania, Zimbabwe, Guinea, Chad, Kenya, Somalia, the Democratic Republic of Congo (DRC), and many others. And let us not forget the terrorist attacks on the US embassies in Nairobi and Dar-el-Salaam a few years ago.

US interests in Africa are not limited to the military but are also economic. For example, the United States imports vast quantities of oil from the African countries, and some of these countries, like Nigeria, Angola, and the Democratic Republic of Congo, are far from being politically stable. Africa should embrace the United States Africa Command, because in the end, it is Africa that will benefit greatly from US security protection. Ask the Europeans, Koreans, and Japanese about this fact.

As we all know, the United States Africa Command Headquarters is currently in Stuttgart, Germany. This is very unfortunate. I think the headquarters of AFRICOM should be based somewhere in Africa. The

United States has its military stationed all over the world without any problems whatsoever. Truthfully, the American GI is a force for good in this troubled world—more so in a very unstable region like Africa.

It is time for Africans to face the real world—a world that is full of evils and opportunists who want to cause more chaos, especially in the poor nations, because that is the only way they prosper and survive. The era of romantic and naive nonalignment once championed and promoted by African leaders is over for good.

The Soviet Union is no longer there, and the West led by the United States is not interested in dominating Africans just for the sake of it. The West will always try to protect its vital interests wherever they may be— but in collaboration with the countries concerned, taking into account the values they believe in, such as democracy, human rights, good governance, free press, rule of law, freedom of religion, and so forth. These values are critically important to Africans, too.[9]

One does not have to look far to realize the critical importance of AFRICOM to African nations, especially those of sub-Saharan Africa, at this time in the history of the continent. The majority of these nations have been facing serious unparalleled domestic political upheaval since they attained independence. Whether in the Democratic

---

[9]   "The United States Africa Command – AFRICOM," *Lazarus' Opinion*, November 2, 2009, http://lazarusopinion.blogspot.com/2009/11/us-africa-command-africom.html.

Republic of Congo (Congo Kinshasa), North and South Sudan, the Ivory Coast, Mali, Guinea, Guinea Bissau, or Zimbabwe, all of them share the same problem—troubling internal political instability. We have just witnessed the insurrection in North Africa, which will have dire long-term consequences for sub-Sahara. What has happened in North Africa could trigger similar uprisings elsewhere in Africa, and that could be even more dangerous to the continent's citizens. If Africans try to rise up against their oppressive governments, there is no doubt whatsoever that many will be murdered—just like we saw in Guinea (West Africa).

It is time for the African countries to admit the obvious: that they simply cannot yet guarantee and foster the security of their citizens without major external assistance. The African nations are very small, weak, and poor. And to top it off, they lack the necessary resources to maintain a large professional military. They cannot afford modern powerful equipment for their ragtag armies. To be honest, African countries do not need these armies. What these countries need, above all, are well-trained and well-equipped police forces and, perhaps, a national guard to maintain law and order—another big problem in sub-Saharan countries.

African leaders do not want to admit that they need foreign military help, mainly because they think that it would look bad and be humiliating for an independent country, among other reasons. But this is total nonsense, because everybody knows the real state of affairs in these nations. As a result of these self-inflicted wounds, African countries spend most of their meager resources on their armies, at the expense of other vital things such as the economy, education, health care, and infrastructure, among many other projects critical to the welfare of their nationals. The result is that these countries are falling further and further behind, with no hope whatsoever of economic development.

Therefore, the involvement of the United States in the defense of sub-Sahara would help these nations to invest less in their security systems and instead invest their limited resources in their economies and important social sectors. And perhaps, most importantly, AFRICOM will help African countries to gain and maintain political stability—a prerequisite for national development and peace. Lack of stability has cost Africa a great deal in terms of foreign capital investments. No country or company wants to invest in a country rife with civil conflicts and mayhem. This surely should be a no-brainer, even for the most backward African leaders.

The military backing of a great power such as the United States will send a positive signal to the world that finally Africa is ready to deal and is open for quantitative business engagements from across the globe.

The presence of AFRICOM in Africa will bring confidence to all foreigners who have enough capital to invest. And these investors will not hesitate to come to sub-Sahara to do business. It is very, very important to point this out. We must look at the case of AFRICOM largely in economic terms, because that is exactly what it should be about—the long-term economic well-being of the continent in the twenty-first century and beyond.

For the last forty or so years, sub-Saharan Africa has been a largely forgotten region to most wealthy investors, especially in the United States, but interestingly also including rich Africans, who decided that investing in their own country would be a waste of their money. Thus, wealthy Africans moved their wealth to safe rich nations in the developed north. All this could change if the Africans were to do the right thing by embracing the presence of the US military on the continent. Africa should learn from the experiences of other regions of the world where the United States' strong military presence brought tremendous economic and other benefits to the people of those countries.

Take, for example, Japan. After the Second World War, the country decided or was forced—depending on one's point of view—to entrust its national security protection to the Americans. We see what has happened to Japan as a result. The same thing happened in Europe. With the United States' economic assistance under the Marshall Plan, combined with the US military to guarantee peace, the Europeans managed to rebuild the continent within a very short period of time. And for those who do not know, the US military is still firmly embedded in both Japan and Europe today.

In all these cases, the United States has acted as a loyal partner and friend to the host nations and has generally refrained from abusing or misusing its military powers in these countries. On the contrary, the United States has been supportive of positive developments in the host countries and has abided by the laws and regulations of its host partners. For those in Africa who still doubt the honest and good intentions of the United States, they should learn from the Europeans, the Japanese, and the Koreans.

Africa, as we have discussed elsewhere, is still dominated by insecurity in one form or another. The majority of the fifty-four independent countries in the African Union (AU) are dangerously unstable. Just look at the current conflicts in the northern and Delta regions of Nigeria. The worsening situation in this country is a telling example of the precarious state of security in African countries. One day a country is peaceful; the next day, the same country is engulfed in a horrific civil conflict. Nigeria is just the latest on a long list of African nations facing various forms of internal insurrection, a situation with which the international community is extremely tired of grappling. Nigeria cannot be ignored because of its importance to the West African region and Africa at large.

For years now, Nigeria has been also dealing with the rebellion of the Ogoni people in the oil-rich Niger Delta, with very limited success. This is due in part to the poor nature of Nigeria's military capabilities and its failed political leadership. The people of Nigeria, who have endured the constant humiliation of the state of affairs in their country, must surely one day rise up to demand a total change for the better in their homeland. It is, at any rate, very clear that Nigeria cannot singlehandedly deal with its internal security problems.

Right now, several African countries, just like Nigeria, are dealing with severe domestic conflicts. On top of these political conflicts, we see the return of traditional military coups—which most people thought a thing of the past in modern Africa. For example, between 2008 and 2012, Africa witnessed coups in Mauritania, Guinea, Niger, Guinea Bissau, and Mali—all in the western part of Africa. These military coups have made life for the citizens worse in these countries. For instance, the coup in Mali took the situation from bad to worse. Mali has been experiencing a very serious rebellion led by the Tuareg rebels, working hand in hand with al-Qaeda in the Islamic Maghreb. The Tuareg rebels, who are Islamists, want to impose sharia law and their brand of Islam on the whole country, and if that is not successful, they want to split Mali into two countries, with them controlling the northern half, or the Azawad Republic as they call it. The tragic coup in Mali gave the rebels the opportunity to do just that, and now these dangerous rebels control the northern part of Mali, which includes the historic city of Timbuktu. Now there are confirmed reports that the Tuaregs have destroyed the ancient Islamic tombs located in Timbuktu, just like the Taliban did in Afghanistan when they were in power.

These rebel groups are a major threat to peace in the entire Maghreb region and other parts of West Africa—with serious political, economic, social, and security consequences. That region is already facing horrendous famine and food shortages caused in large part by the drought and the failure of governments in the region to foresee and plan for such occurrences.

The involvement of al-Qaeda in Africa should be the most worrying development considering the damage this rebel organization has done across the globe. Al-Qaeda leaders know that Africa is a very soft target because of the weak and unstable government structures of the countries and the continent. The countries of Africa have very ineffective and disorganized armies, which are no match for the well-disciplined and battle-tested al-Qaeda operatives. Case in point, in Nigeria, al-Qaeda is believed to be supporting the Boko Haram rebels, who have declared war in northern Nigeria and are responsible for the horrendous killings of Christians in the region.

The Nigerian army, as discussed previously, has so far failed to contain the deteriorating situation, and the government is not willing to bring in an outside force to deal with Boko Haram and its foreign backers such as al-Qaeda. What we are seeing in Nigeria is also playing out in other countries in the African continent. As we have already discussed, in Mali, the Tuareg rebels, backed by another group known as the Ansar Dine, now in control of northern Mali, are being supported by al-Qaeda in the Islamic Maghreb. Al-Qaeda is there because the state of Mali is weak—just like Nigeria and other countries in Africa. Mali, as previously mentioned, is now in danger of being split into two nations, with al-Qaeda finding yet another safe haven in northern Mali. This situation must not be allowed to stand.

The government of Mali, or whatever passes as the legitimate authority in the country, must ask the US government for direct intervention. The threat of al-Qaeda is real in the region, just like in Somalia, the Great Lakes region, and the Horn of Africa area. Some people, especially leaders in Africa, mistakenly think that al-Qaeda and its many affiliates are only a threat to Western countries. This is a very careless underestimation of the security dangers posed by these international terrorist groups. Africans must never forget the terrorist attacks in Nairobi and Dar-el-Salaam that took the lives of hundreds of innocent Kenyans, Tanzanians, and Americans. And those behind the attacks have since been identified as al-Qaeda affiliate operatives in the two countries. Interestingly, some of their cadres have also admitted that they had something to do with the attacks.

In the neighboring Somalia, the rebel group al-Shabaab is also known to be heavily backed by al-Qaeda. In Somalia's case, al-Qaeda found a very safe base, because that country is really a failed state and has been without a national government since the 1980s. Al-Qaeda knows that if al-Shabaab prevails in Somalia, then that country will be their permanent base of operations across that region of Africa—a very frightening prospect indeed. The fact that al-Shabaab is as strong as it is in Somalia should be a sobering warning to all that this organization will do whatever it takes to achieve its stated goal of spreading its radical brand of Islam, by any means necessary, across the globe.

We are now dealing with a situation in Africa in which some countries are losing or have already lost their national sovereignty to these international terrorist groups and their local collaborators. The loss of sovereignty in Somalia is the critical reason why the Horn of Africa is now such a dangerous area. If Somalia were a properly functioning state, then al-Shabaab rebels would not have seized that nation and turned it into a haven for international terrorists and a safe base for modern-day pirates who have now turned the waters of Somalia into a dangerous area for international maritime activities. This is totally unacceptable, and is one more concrete reason why Africa needs a permanent US military presence in the continent.

The enemies of Africa, within or without, know that a permanent US presence in the continent would be a major threat to their existence and to their impunity with regard to having created chaos and insecurity in Africa. With a permanent US presence, the sorry state of affairs will be brought to an end and attention turned to what is most important for the hapless people of Africa—the economy.

The African people want their security to be guaranteed. They also want to go about doing business without the constant disruptions often caused by their governments and, of course now, by the dangerous forces from outside their countries. It is time for a major foreign power such as the United States to come in and work with these fragile African governments to establish true constitutional governance, peaceful coexistence, and above all genuine economic prosperity.

Peace and prosperity are the only things that will restore the confidence of the African people in their governments and nations. The benefits of peace, unity, and prosperity in Africa will be immense. For example, the ingenuity and abundant optimism of the African people will be greatly rekindled, and that in turn will spur all sorts of positive developments throughout the continent.

With the US Armed Forces working cooperatively with their African partners to prevent insecurity, soon the millions of Africans who are living in the diaspora will start to create businesses in their former countries back in Africa. In other words, the domino effects of peace and prosperity in the continent will be so overwhelming that for the first time in almost a century, the region will be the main center of attention and perhaps admiration.

That is why, for those who really care about the long-term future of Africa, it is now your turn to speak up forcefully and work hard to sell the positive things that will benefit the African citizens as a result of AFRICOM's coming to the continent. And for those leaders and opinion makers in Africa who are obstructing or openly campaigning against AFRICOM, they better get on board or step aside. All they want is to destroy the one flicker of hope for Africa. It has been a long time coming—therefore, let this be the African century.

However, all these good things will remain a pipe dream until all the senseless conflicts are stamped out in every country and all the regions of Africa. We have already discussed the enormous problems in the western Africa nations and Somalia in the east. But the conflicts in eastern Africa are not limited to Somalia and the Horn of Africa.

In the Great Lakes and central regions, the continent is grappling with the growing conflicts in the newly independent South Sudan, the continuing war in the eastern Democratic Republic of Congo (DRC), and the major threats still posed by the remnants of the Lord's Resistance Army of Joseph Kony, now based somewhere in the Central African Republic (CAR). Joseph Kony has eluded capture for years now and still continues to commit atrocities across several nations in Central Africa. That was why it came as a relief when President Obama decided to authorize one hundred US military personnel to go and act as advisers to the Ugandan army—so as to effectively take on Joseph Kony and, perhaps, finally capture or kill him. This is the kind of cooperation and assistance Africa badly needs from the United States, and this is why AFRICOM is critically important for the continent.

Then there is the civil war in the eastern Democratic Republic of Congo, which shows no signs of coming to an end. The DRC, which, by its sheer size, is the largest country in Africa, is also perhaps the most disorganized and poorest in the continent. This instability in the DRC threatens the security of the entire eastern and central regions of Africa.

In southern Africa, we have the tragic political thuggery in Zimbabwe caused in large part by the leadership of President Robert Mugabe and his ZANU–PF Party, which has forced thousands of Zimbabweans to flee to neighboring nations. This, in turn, has put an enormous burden on these countries. This refugee situation is taking place at a time when these countries are dealing with their own economic and other problems.

Zimbabwe was once a very promising African country with an economic prowess second only to that of the Republic of South Africa. With Robert Mugabe still firmly entrenched in power, and with the productive people of Zimbabwe, especially the White commercial farmers, still leaving Zimbabwe remains a very serious threat to peace in the southern region.

With all these critical security challenges the African nations are facing, one would have expected Africa to be highly enthusiastic about hosting AFRICOM. However, this has not been the case. Instead, African countries are not showing any positive signs or much interest in bringing the headquarters of AFRICOM to the continent. Let me make one thing extremely clear: Africa is missing a huge opportunity. I really don't understand the thinking of African leaders. We all know that the sub-Saharan countries are very poor economically, in part because of their internal instability and the lack of overall security in the subcontinent. Therefore, one simply wonders why the continent has not jumped on this rare opportunity, the likes of which Africa does not often receive. Other countries and regions that have benefited a great deal from the guaranteed security protection of the United States are genuinely surprised at the hesitancy of the Africans to welcome the permanent presence of the US Army on the continent.

There are some countries in Africa that should be able to host an AFRICOM headquarters without major political difficulties. Some of these countries are Botswana, Ghana, South Africa, Kenya, Uganda, Djibouti, and Rwanda. These countries are generally stable, and their citizens are not known to be anti-American in any serious way. Interestingly, Djibouti, Kenya, and Uganda already have a lengthy experience in collaborating with the US military.

The case for basing the AFRICOM headquarters in Africa is so compelling that I call on all those who care about the long-term future of Africa to start a massive campaign for AFRICOM to find a base on the continent. The Germans do not mind temporarily allowing AFRICOM to be based there, but this critical military force is meant for Africa, and therefore it must reside on the continent. Surely, presidents such as Yoweri Museveni of Uganda and Paul Kagame of Rwanda, along with a few others, are astute enough to understand the importance of the US military involvement in Africa, especially in this century. This must be the century in which Africa becomes a major force for good in the world and an equal player in the international economic system.

In order to achieve this goal, African leaders know that the continent will need more than just kind words from their important partners in the West. In order to start the long march out of the dire situation the continent has remained in for the last half a century, a period that most would agree was totally wasted, Africa will need support. US leaders have reiterated that the US military is not going to replace or dominate the African armies, but work cooperatively as friends and partners to maintain peace and order in the continent.

This is how seriously the United States takes its relations with Africa now, as opposed to in the past. The Africans must be extremely pleased by the confidence the Americans are putting in the continent, especially sub-Sahara. We all know that the United States doesn't have to do this, but it is willing to put its mighty army in Africa because the American people care about the people of Africa. It is time for the African countries to come up with completely new policies regarding their engagement with the West.

The postcolonial and Cold War mind-set is not helping. Instead, it is hindering the development of Africa. This negativity toward the West is prevalent in sub-Sahara, with the result being that the entire region is the poorest on the face of the earth. African leaders must stop implementing foreign policies that are in total disregard of their vital interests, because this irresponsible nationalism from the time of independence to the present time has not gotten Africa anywhere. Africa has been relegated to the very bottom on almost every issue, and its voice, even collectively, is generally disregarded by the nations that matter most at this time in our history.

5

The United States' Generous Response to Africa's HIV/AIDS Epidemic

The acronyms HIV and AIDS have indelibly become very powerfully synonymous with Africa, especially sub-Sahara. Nobody seems to be sure about how this epidemic came to be so heavily associated with sub-Sahara. Nevertheless, this deadly disease is most certainly the most serious threat to the health of the African people in modern history and a very bad curse upon the continent. The majority of Africans are still scratching their heads trying to come to terms with this horrific epidemic. The problem is so overwhelming that most poor African nations are simply unable to deal with it. As a result, some countries have regrettably given up any attempts to try to contain the spread of the disease.

The origin of HIV/AIDS is not very clear. There is controversy regarding in which country or countries the disease first appeared. Most non-African experts strongly believe that it began in sub-Saharan Africa. However, this view is not shared by a large percentage of Africans, who believe that HIV/AIDS originated somewhere else. But, as usual, it is the Africans who are being blamed for the epidemic. These are, of course, merely academic arguments. It does not matter where HIV/AIDS originated; the truth is that these suspicions have been very unhelpful in the fight against this epidemic.

It is extremely hard to quantify exactly how many black Africans have died from HIV/AIDS. But most experts seem to agree that more than thirty million Africans have perished as a result of this terrible disease. We must, however, keep in mind that it would have been worse if it hadn't been for the massive assistance the African nations have received from developed countries, especially the USA. The problems of HIV/AIDS in Africa vary from country to country, depending on the level of infection and the standard of health care services available. In much of Africa, the provision of quality health care services has never been a top governmental priority.

The majority of African countries have few health care professionals such as doctors and nurses in virtually all areas of medical service. The few who are there are forced to work under the most severe circumstances, including in dilapidated buildings with ancient obsolete equipment and shortages of nearly all kinds of drugs. These unpalatable conditions have caused the exodus of thousands of trained medical professionals out of Africa. They've gone on to advanced countries where conditions are much better and, most importantly, they earn more money—something all African countries have failed to provide. As a result, when the HIV/AIDS epidemic broke, all the affected countries in sub-Sahara were caught completely unprepared. Even worse, most of them are still in the same situation today.

The HIV/AIDS epidemic is not a problem in Africa alone or just limited to that continent. The epidemic is wreaking havoc in other nations as well, outside of Africa. It is a global problem, though the problem is much more frightening in Africa. The astronomical level of infections; the number of deaths, orphans, and widows; the loss of the professional class and other working people—the tragedy is much, much higher in Africa than on any other continent. Very few African countries have stepped up to confront this killer disease. This is because most African regimes don't have the resources required for taking on such a huge emergent problem, or else they are so disorganized that they cannot deal with the problem.

This has created a situation whereby most of the Africans carrying the disease are left to fend for themselves—and that usually means needless death. The HIV/AIDS victims in other countries, especially the developed nations, are not dying of the disease the way people are doing in Africa. The main reason is the quality of health care the victims are getting and the critical drugs, such as antiretrovirals, available at affordable costs to them. In most developed countries, HIV/AIDS patients can generally afford to acquire the expensive drugs, or else their governments provide them with the drugs. This is obviously not the case in sub-Sahara, where people are very poor and their governments are in no position to do anything to help them.

The outbreak of HIV/AIDS could not have come at a worse time for sub-Sahara. Most of the countries in the region, especially those most affected by the epidemic, were already undergoing serious political upheavals of one form or another. Countries such as Rwanda and Uganda were in turmoil, causing the problem of HIV/AIDS to rank low on their domestic policy priorities. In the meantime, the disease was spreading like wildfire and taking the lives of countless citizens.

By the time, for example, the government of Uganda started to take the HIV/AIDS epidemic seriously, the problem had become too big for Uganda to handle singlehandedly. However, this does not mean that Uganda didn't try. This small East African country was perhaps one of the first countries in the world to credibly put together a concrete and measurable program of action against HIV/AIDS. The ABC (Abstinence, Be Faithful, and Condoms) program was recognized globally as being one of the best of that era, and it helped to spur other countries to establish their own programs. It was acknowledged at the time, as it is even today by governments in the West, especially the USA, and by international organizations dealing with the AIDS epidemic, that Uganda actually did a great job to combat the killer disease. However, it was too little to make a huge difference.

Uganda, just like all other African nations, is still not capable of dealing with a problem of this magnitude. Let us remember that these countries have failed to put an end to malaria, tuberculosis, and other common diseases that have been completely eradicated in other countries. People around the world just do not understand why sub-Saharan Africa is ground zero for HIV/AIDS and some people are even thinking the unthinkable—which is that before this disease is brought under complete control, perhaps half of the African population will die of the disease!

This is not being alarmist. It is what some people, including well-meaning experts, are contemplating. Will such a thing ever come to pass? No one can predict for sure what will happen in sub-Sahara in the years ahead. However, the very good news is that Africa is not fighting against this disease alone. There are many nations and organizations that are already helping the African people who have contracted or are carrying HIV/AIDS. The outside efforts have helped to contain the high rate of death among both adults and children born with the disease.

In *Cordial Relations between Africa and the United States in the Twenty-First Century: How the United States Can Help to Transform the Continent*, I want to highlight especially the assistance of the United States of America provided to the people of sub-Sahara regarding the HIV/AIDS epidemic. The help from the United States, although a bit late in this instance, nevertheless was the best thing for all those who were suffering and dying of HIV/AIDS, due in part to extremely poor medical services. I say the help came a bit late because the disease was at its peak in much of sub-Sahara in the early to late 1980s, the period during which countless numbers of Africans contracted HIV/AIDS and most of them died.

The intervention of the US government in the fight against HIV/AIDS in Africa was by no means the first of such assistance provided by the USA. Different American charity organizations and other well-wishers were already doing their part to assist the AIDS victims in sub-Sahara. However, the intervention of the US government was on such a scale that it was bound to make a huge impact almost immediately in the lives of the AIDS victims in all the targeted countries in the continent. The majority of the people, particularly those in sub-Sahara, had not expected the kind of assistance the US government proposed, usually of the magnitude given to the nations of Europe, Asia, the Middle East, and South America, but not Africa.

For most of us, the first time we heard about the US intention to aid the African people in their struggle against the AIDS tragedy was during the State of the Union Address in January 2003. In his speech, President George W. Bush promised to put a huge amount of the United States' resources toward aiding the fight against HIV/AIDS globally. The president, in his State of the Union Address, stated, "I ask the Congress to commit $15 billion over the five years to turn the tide against AIDS in the most afflicted nations of Africa and the Caribbean."[10]

Following President Bush's appeal in his State of the Union Address, in May 2003, the US Congress approved, and President Bush signed into law, the United States Leadership Against HIV/AIDS,

---

[10] "Funding for HIV and AIDS," Avert, last updated August 15, 2017, http://www.avert.org/pepfar.htm.

Tuberculosis, and Malaria Act of 2003.[11] This program is widely known as the President's Emergency Plan for AIDS Relief (PEPFAR). Under this law, the US government committed to spending up to $15 billion over five years, mostly in sub-Saharan Africa but also in the Caribbean nations. This kind of generosity was unheard of. For the United States to commit this astronomical sum of money to the Africans, of all people, was hard to believe at first. But there it was, the president of the United States of America telling the world that the African people also matter and, therefore, the great country of the United States, and really the world, must not just sit back and let them die of HIV/AIDS.

President Bush surprised all the skeptics of the United States' true intentions in Africa after he signed the PEPFAR legislation in May 2003. When he had become the forty-third president of the United States, all experts on global matters had written him off as some kind of lightweight on international affairs, especially when it came to Africa. Therefore, it came as a surprise to all of us when this same president became the champion of trying to come up with a major health care strategy to help those who were dying of AIDS in Africa. Nobody expected President Bush to propose this massive assistance for Africa, but he did it.

The unfortunate thing is that President Bush's great humanitarian initiative has not been highly appreciated by the Africans, especially the continent's leaders who have collectively done a very miserable job of taking care of their citizens, even amid an extreme health care emergency such as this. Think of what would have happened to AIDS victims in sub-Sahara without this massive US financial assistance! They would have been deprived of the antiretroviral drugs because of the high cost. But with the money from the United States, the drugs

---

[11]   Ibid.

were highly subsidized, thereby enabling poor Africans to afford them, thanks to President Bush and the US Congress.

The $15 billion appropriated for Africa and the Caribbean was the largest amount of assistance ever allotted to these poor nations. That amount of money is more than the combined national budgets of almost all sub-Saharan countries selected to receive the initial assistance. If we look at the most afflicted countries in sub-Sahara at that period—Botswana, the Ivory Coast, Ethiopia, Kenya, Mozambique, Namibia, Nigeria, Rwanda, South Africa, Tanzania, Uganda, and Zambia—in all of them, with the exception perhaps of Botswana, the governments spent very little on HIV/AIDS and the patients were left to fend for themselves without any credible medical care. A lot of Africans died because they could not afford the very expensive drugs needed to prolong their lives or to prevent the epidemic from spreading.

The most unfortunate thing about the AIDS situation in sub-Saharan Africa was that the African governments never quite treated or regarded this deadly epidemic as the most serious threat to the very future of the continent, which was yet another sign of the neglect and rot in sub-Sahara. The African regimes provided pathetically little or virtually no budgetary provisions for the fight against HIV/AIDS in their respective countries. No African nation, for example, declared a state of emergency in order to heighten their citizens' awareness of this killer disease and make it abundantly clear that this epidemic was going to be one of the biggest health crises in postindependence Africa. Some African governments even tried to deny the very existence of HIV/AIDS in their countries.

One of the most prominent governments to doubt or seriously question the existence of HIV/AIDS as it is known was the Republic of South Africa under Thabo Mbeki. This was the one president who was perhaps the most enlightened leader of his generation in Africa.

President Mbeki turned out to be a major disappointment when it came to dealing with the HIV/AIDS crisis in his country. It remains a mystery what caused Thabo Mbeki to resort to denying the obvious. One can only guess that he perhaps had been badly advised by his science officials about the deadly HIV/AIDS.

While President Thabo Mbeki was questioning the existence of HIV/AIDS in South Africa, in Uganda, as we mentioned earlier, the government of Yoweri Museveni, to its credit, took a very different course. At the height of the HIV/AIDS epidemic, the government of Uganda decided to embrace the policy of complete transparency about the disease and accepted the fact that HIV/AIDS was real and therefore ought to be dealt with openly and seriously. This policy of transparency allowed Uganda, with the assistance of the international community and especially the United States, to deal with this disease much more effectively, which eventually led to the improvement of the situation in that country. Uganda's experience was, of course, unique. Therefore, it cannot be replicated exactly everywhere in Africa. Nevertheless, other African countries must try to learn something from Uganda's experience.

The people of the United States are always ready to assist those who are genuinely striving to improve their living conditions and to lift their countries out of abject poverty. The US aid to Africa will continue if the continent proves that it means business, turns away from wasting its meager resources, and starts to invest in priority national sectors such as health care. The United States wants to supplement but not to replace Africa's own efforts. While the generosity of the American people is applauded, it is now time for sub-Saharan Africa to prove that it can also be self-sufficient and can ably do great things such as handling the HIV/AIDS pandemic.

6

Education and Cultural Cooperation

In the early years of political independence in Africa, the United States played a significant role in developing the education sectors in the then young African countries. That was, of course, when the hopes and aspirations were still very high for the long-term prospects of these African countries, especially for their citizens. As we all now know, all those rosy and unrealistic hopes were dashed almost immediately, just a few years after independence.

Having said that, I do not want *Cordial Relations between Africa and the United States in the Twenty-First Century* to be about reliving or rehashing the numerous mistakes African countries have endured with devastating consequences over many years. What is important here is to stress the idea that if Africa is to have any chance of a promising future, the education of its citizens must be placed at the center of everything. This sounds very simple and is something every nation must do as a matter of course, especially for those who are not Africans, but in Africa, this is not so simple for many reasons.

First, it is worth reminding people that the European colonialists left the African countries with an extremely poor and woefully inadequate education sector. Most of the newly independent countries had just a handful of primary schools, secondary schools, and universities. Actually, the majority of the countries, especially in sub-Sahara, had no institutions of higher learning! In most cases, universities and colleges were established to cater to whole regions of Africa. For example, Makerere College in Kampala, Uganda, was the main center of higher education in the East African region. Just imagine one institution of higher learning for the millions of eager young Africans burning with the ambition for a university education. The European colonialists who did this to the poor Africans were not serious about the future prosperity and happiness of the African people. It is very hard to understand the reasons why the highly intelligent and civilized Europeans did this harm to the Africans, the very people they supposedly intended to civilize, modernize, and organize into national states.

The whole bad situation was then left to inexperienced and very ill-educated African leaders to grapple with. Almost all of them failed right from the start. For these new countries, instead of embarking on the establishment of primary schools, secondary schools, and various institutions of higher learning on a grand scale, to help kick-start the development of these countries, the African leaders began to waste their meager resources on the building of security forces. Large sums of scarce money went toward building military camps, recruiting soldiers, and purchasing weapons. While this negative trend was taking place in much of sub-Saharan countries, over in Asia, the new nations there—also former colonies of the European powers—were already busy investing wisely in the education of their citizens. As a result, sixty or so years later, today Asia is a region on the verge of overtaking the OECD countries. The African countries south of the Sahara would be in the same economic situation as the Asian countries if they had spent their resources on vital sectors such as education, health care, infrastructure, and agriculture—instead of military buildups and, of course, the overwhelmingly corrupt and incompetent leadership.

It has already been mentioned in this writing that the twenty-first century must be Africa's century. And I am willing to predict, optimistically, that this century will be Africa's. However, African countries and African peoples must start doing things very differently. The old ways have not worked and will never work. Consequently, the sub-Sahara must get back to the fundamentals. In other words, the region needs to get the foundation of development right this time around, and then the rest will fall into place. By this, of course, I mean really getting education right. All the ills of the African nations will not be righted overnight, but education is the critical key to unlocking the ingenuity of the sub-Saharan people.

Although Africa is at the very bottom compared to every other place in the world, and most development experts agree on this, the situation is not hopeless. This is because some countries in the region are performing a bit better than the majority.

However, in much of sub-Sahara, the education sector still exists largely because of the international NGOs and the foreign governments giving aid, and in most cases even helping to run the education departments.

I feel very strongly about the education of Africans, because we know for sure that the citizens of African countries want to see their respective nations advance and grow to become economically secure. That is why I believe the one nation that can help to rebuild Africa's education is the United States of America. If the American people really care about the future of the continent—which I believe they do—then this is another sector in which the United States should invest, without a single hesitation. We have seen what US resources can do when put to good use, for example, in the case of the HIV/AIDS epidemic in Africa. The US assistance program popularly known as the President's Emergency Plan for AIDS Relief (PEPFAR) has, to date, saved the lives of millions of poor Africans who otherwise would be dead of HIV/AIDS.

Now it is a matter of education. The United States is helping to keep a lot of Africans alive. Therefore, the focus should now be concentrated on guaranteeing the long-term well-being of the region. As we saw with the case of HIV/AIDS, African countries still lack the resources required to overhaul and completely rebuild their education sectors. And as we know all too well, rebuilding an education sector requires more than just the services of Peace Corps volunteers. It will take enormous capital investments and political will to undertake this project in Africa. But for the sake of the African people, it must be done. The burden has become too heavy for the developed countries to constantly intervene to bail this or that country in sub-Saharan African out of the numerous crises they always face. From famine, health, and starvation to civil wars and other inhuman degradations, the African people are always at the mercy of the unpredictable natural calamities and are the victims of their failed states.

However, there is hope in education. A well-managed and well-funded education sector would most certainly change the state of sub-Sahara within a decade or two. Helping the Africans receive well-targeted and meaningful education would be more beneficial to the majority in the continent than giving aid directly to the dysfunctional African governments. It is a well-known fact that the financial assistance that has gone to the African nations in the past couple of decades has been mostly wasted or has just disappeared, leaving the recipient countries in virtually the same condition year after year, with no hope for millions of Africans.

As a result, the argument and the appeal in this particular case are both different. Let us put education at the core of African's transformation and renaissance, and move forward in the twenty-first century with the total backing and assistance of the USA. Yes, the United States now has huge domestic challenges, especially with budgetary and other constrains. However, this cause is just as critical as WWII, in which the United States was called upon and generously responded to those challenges—and the rest, as they say, is history. I believe the American people can help Africa rebuild and thereby help create a better future.

As we have already seen elsewhere, the United States has always assisted, and still is assisting, various African countries in many ways, large and small. But education, above all else, is what will guarantee the future of sub-Sahara for centuries to come, and that would be a very good outcome for the world, especially with regard to African-US relations.

Let us always keep in mind that the USA has helped Africa before in the development of its education sector. Now the USA must do even more, in part because of the regression that has taken place on the continent in the last couple of decades. One hopes that the more Africans become well educated and literate, the better it will be for the countries of the region, and perhaps most importantly, the people will rise up and reject the present situation they are forced to live amid. They will, hopefully, demand a much higher standard of everything, such as governance, economy, social conditions, and transparency, and they themselves will become better political, business, civic, and professional managers of their homelands.

This author is not asking the United States to do what it is not capable of doing. However, he is requesting the greatest country in the world undertake what will transform sub-Sahara once and for all—and education is the key foundation in that process. How to go about doing this is really simple. Working with selected African governments and the international NGOs that currently operate in various African nations, the USA can take stock of the number of primary schools, secondary schools, and institutions of higher learning currently available in the chosen African countries or the entire subregion. My educated guess is that there are not many at all. Just take one example. The majority of African countries have, at best, one or two universities and colleges, and most countries have none at all. Therefore, these countries depend on other nations, especially those in the developed north and in Asia, for the higher education of their citizens as part of the economic development assistance offered by those rich countries.

So then, by developing and raising the standard of Africa's education sector, the USA could change this pattern. And the best way to start is by building and equipping more schools, particularly primary and secondary, and then technical or vocational, schools. In the 1960s, US aid helped to build some secondary schools in Uganda and in other African countries. Take it from me: those were the best investments the United States made in Africa.

Also keep in mind that in the 1960s, the African population was still very small, and the social and economic conditions in the newly independent African nations were still generally good. Today, the population of African countries has exploded to almost a billion people, but the number of institutions of all levels of education has not kept up with the pace of population growth. The huge population increase has compounded sub-Sahara's already enormous developmental challenges. Therefore, revamping Africa's moribund education sector will require enormous capital investment from the United States.

The positive thing with the United States is that it has the public and private funds for such a big project. The US Congress must see this venture for what it is—something that will ensure the future prosperity and stability of sub-Sahara. Helping to set up enough schools in the region will be in the best long-term interests of the

USA. This time, Africa desperately needs the total commitment of the USA in its struggle for development. At the same time, America's vast number of private philanthropists and think tanks must refocus their attention on this extremely vital undertaking. Groups such as the Rockefeller Foundation, the Bill and Melinda Gates Foundation, and the Clinton Global Initiative should invest more of their resources in the education of the African people.

Some of these private groups are already operating in some sub-Saharan countries. For example, the Clinton Global Initiative (CGI) is one of the premier US NGOs already doing great works in sub-Saharan Africa. And its contributions to the general welfare of the African people have been tremendous. Whether it is in the fight against HIV/AIDS or promoting economic growth actions, the CGI is at the forefront of the efforts to lift Africa from the depths of despair. This is exactly the type of US assistance *Cordial Relations between Africa and the United States in the Twenty-First Century* is about. Other major US NGOs should follow the Clinton example, but this time focus on the education projects, because these will have a critical long-term impact on the future of Africa. I cannot emphasize this point enough. If the right thing is not done this time round, then we can forget about Africa becoming self-reliant, or an equal and confident partner of the USA, for many years to come.

US universities and colleges must also play their part. The majority of these universities and colleges are very wealthy. Therefore, they can afford to invest some of their resources in the development of Africa's higher education. In this instance, I am thinking about American universities, both public and private, extending their branches to sub-Sahara, with courses or programs limited to vital areas relevant to Africa's short- and long-term economic development. Subjects such as agriculture, education, engineering, medicine, accounting, public administration, business management, and sciences are the most important areas of study for Africa, especially at this stage of these countries' economic development. And above all, these programs must be offered at a heavily subsidized tuition rate; otherwise, the main purpose of putting these institutions in sub-Sahara would be lost. You want the courses to be affordable so that the poor African students are able to pay for them.

As I have discussed repeatedly, Africa's problems are so numerous that sometimes one doesn't know where to begin. We want to emphasize education, but Africans are also starving, and the health problems related to malnutrition have grown exponentially, year after year, in this most needy region of the world. The chronic shortage of food to feed the ever-growing population in sub-Sahara is becoming a crisis—which, interestingly, nobody is speaking about loudly. African governments, have for decades, paid very little attention to this tragedy, while the African masses continue to deal with the insecurity that comes with the shortage of food. That is why, in this struggle to lift Africans from abject poverty, there must be a concerted effort to invest in the training of more agricultural experts, with the single-minded goal of attacking hunger by hugely increasing the production of food. Moving from subsistence to commercial or mechanized agriculture requires that the skills of African farmers be enhanced.

The entire world knows that US agriculture is the finest and most productive. The United States alone can feed the whole world for years. Why is this so? Only about 2 percent of Americans are farmers! The difference here is that US farmers are highly skilled, with many of them highly educated and also landowners. This is another area where the United States can help Africa. I don't want to make this sound as if it is very simple. No, it is much more complicated than meets the eye, and that is why it must start with education, which means raising a new generation of Africans to become productive farmers. The age of subsistence agriculture in sub-Saharan Africa must come to an end for the sake of the people there.

Better and more relevant education will gradually make Africans better political leaders, military leaders, bureaucrats, farmers, entrepreneurs, and incubators of vital innovation needed for the region's economic growth for years to come. Where is Africa now in terms of scientific innovation? As far as we know, not very far. Take the most important scientific development of our times—the IT revolution. African leaders, as usual, are not even paying attention to this new engine of economic activity—the way that Asian leaders, for instance, are doing.

The sub-Sahara, as we speak, is already too far behind in virtually all areas of high technology, and now we can add to this the modern and perhaps the most powerful innovation of our era, the internet, and all other innovations that have developed around it. This is the engine behind the fantastic economic growth in some of the newly emerging markets and developed economies. Just ponder the greatness of the companies such as Google, Yahoo, Amazon, AOL, Facebook, and Twitter, plus the huge benefits they have brought to the USA. Right now, only a small number of people in sub-Sahara have real access to the internet. The majority of African people don't even know what a computer looks like. This is without doubt a major hindrance to sub-Sahara's economic growth. The internet revolution is making the biggest economic impact in this century. Africa must not be marginalized and left behind yet again. We have already pointed out that Africa missed the Industrial Revolution; unfortunately it is happening again with this IT revolution.

This is exactly why education is critical to the effort of retooling and transforming Africa. The United States must help to train engineers in the IT field and provide sub-Saharan countries with all the necessary IT equipment to stop these countries from falling even farther behind the rest of the world. Whether it is in agriculture, high technology, or any other human endeavor, the story of sub-Sahara has been one of a total disappointment so far. This sorry state of affairs must not be allowed to continue any longer. Empowering the majority of African people through positive and well-targeted education will bring to an end the wrenching misery the people of the region have endured for the past few centuries. The African regimes are not going to come out and admit that they have let down their countries. But we all know the unacceptable conditions that are prevailing in the continent right now.

The United States and its universities must help to prepare the next generation of bright African scholars through an enhanced and improved program of visitation under the auspices of the Fulbright scholars and also grant more doctoral scholarships. Scholars are needed now more than ever to teach in the new universities and colleges, as well as to help strengthen the run-down older institutions of higher learning in the sub-Saharan region.

In other parts of the world, education is taken for granted. Not so in Africa, because this is still the region where education is limited to a very few segments of society, especially higher education. This situation is not sustainable any longer. Africa must break away from this stagnation and underdevelopment now. This appeal to the United States is a call to arms—a call to the richest country on earth to do whatever it takes to rescue the people who are falling farther and farther behind in virtually all aspects of modern life, especially in economic development.

Africans are people with rich cultural traditions that are admired globally. These people are capable of adapting and learning new ways of doing things, if properly guided. Let us keep in mind that these are the same people who were brutally colonized and subjected to all sorts of inhuman degradation but somehow managed to survive.

However, the psychological damage is still there, to some extent. We must never minimize the psychological wounds sustained by black Africans—as this is partly why they are in the state they are in.

Sometimes the people of Africa and the conditions on the ground are seriously misunderstood in the United States because of the portrayal of the sub-Sahara by the Western media. We know that there are a lot of terrible things being perpetrated in the region, and they must be reported. However, there are also some good things happening in Africa, and they also must be covered. The US media, particularly, must report the good and the bad in Africa and not just the bad. That is why the emphasis of this chapter is also on enhanced cultural cooperation between the United States and Africa. This cooperation will help to change the negative image of Africa in the United States and vice versa.

The most constructive way to deepen cooperation between Africa and the United States is through cultural exchanges. It has already been noted elsewhere in this reading that this generation of Africans love a lot of things about the United States, especially its popular culture. Young Africans love America's movies, music, and clothes. To this generation of Africans, everything that comes from the United States is classy and highly admired. This is really good. If the majority of American people were exposed to Africa's popular culture, they would love a lot of it and probably would want to enjoy some of those things.

The American people know very little about this aspect of Africa because general public knowledge of things in sub-Sahara is intensely focused on the negative—on strife, corruption, famine, military coups, and so forth. You rarely see the rich cultural traditions of Africa—the old and the modern, including the exquisite African art sometimes referred to as primitive art—being discussed in American media. These are Africa's traditions, but they tend to be overlooked because

77

of the sad history of Africa and the colossal failures of postcolonial nation-states.

These postcolonial nation-states have done a very poor job of marketing the great things of Africa to the American audience. By this I do not mean selling coffee, tea, or gold; I mean relentlessly exposing what is good in sub-Sahara to the people of the United States. The African media, almost all of which are government controlled, are in no position to report to the world, especially the United States, the positive side of the continent. The media in Africa are still generally weak and lack the necessary resources for global coverage like, say, the media in the United States, Europe, and Asia have.

Therefore, the task in this instance must rest with the experienced, resourceful US media to do justice to the events of sub-Sahara in their reporting. This is not demanding too much from the US media.

Let us briefly look back to post–World War II Europe. The portrayal of a devastated Europe after the war by the American media helped to get the US Congress to grant a massive amount of aid to the countries of Europe, with the overwhelming support of the American people. Interestingly, the tradition of helping nations in need has continued to this day. And look at what has been the result—a much, much closer partnership between the United States and western Europe for the past sixty or so years. The economic benefits accrued to both regions have been enormous, and their cooperation keeps expanding.

Now the United States must do the same thing with its African partners. The poor African region today is the continent of the future. Therefore, it is in the Americans' best long-term national interest to work to step up the relationship. African regimes, especially the few good ones—along with media and popular entertainers—must also play their part to strengthen the partnership. But as we all know, the African side is definitely going to fall short for the reasons we have already discussed. Consequently, the Americans will have to do more to bring the two sides much closer. The role played by the American media will be critical to this effort. And how is the effective way to do this?

First of all, the American media must start taking Africa more seriously than they have been doing since independence. For example, the number of US media representatives in sub-Sahara is so small that it begs the question of why. Surely, the US media can do better than that. How many media houses in the United States have permanent correspondents in half the African countries—say like the BBC in London? None! Some media houses have just one reporter covering the whole of Africa. NPR has, perhaps, two or three bureaus on the entire continent right now. The *New York Times* is no better; nor are the major TV networks.

This is inexcusable. Surely Africa has more news to cover that would be of interest to the American public. This is not being hard on the American media, which I have a high regard for. The reason for my major focus on the media is that I know their power to shape public attitudes and opinions. And as we move forward, we want the attitude to be favorable and supportive of what we want to accomplish in Africa.

We definitely want the American people to know about the struggles experienced by the ever-growing number of African businesspeople and their achievements. And we also want to educate Americans about the few successful commercial farmers in the region who labor with very little governmental help and virtually no loans for expansion and growth. Just imagine American farmers going without credit or US government subsidies. This is the real plight of African farmers, but luckily they persist and continue to till the land and employ a few of their fellow citizens.

These are the things the American people should know about. The American media should also let the country know about the few—and they really are only a few—African homegrown doctors (MDs) who are courageous enough to stay and work in sub-Sahara. These doctors sacrifice everything to work in the region under the most horrendous circumstances. These doctors are the true heroes. They deserve credit and the admiration of the American people.

Another thing I feel very strongly about is the small, but important, independent media in sub-Saharan Africa. Most people outside Africa do not know that there are independent journalists operating in Africa. Unlike in the United States, in Africa the private media companies are severely persecuted by their governments, and many journalists are either jailed or killed just for reporting on the things the governments want to keep secret, such as corruption and all other governmental failures.

American journalists based in Africa must talk about this vital industry and correctly inform the American people that private media exists in Africa but is constantly being attacked and strangled by the dictatorial regimes in the region—all under the pretext of preserving national unity and security. In the United States, the freedom of the press is firmly enshrined in the US Constitution. The governments of the United States have always abided by this provision without question. This is not the case in Africa. That is why this unique American tradition must be cultivated in Africa too.

The US press and other organizations must become the champions of the struggling independent media in Africa. The region needs freedom of press more than other developing countries because of the high rate of governmental abuses that usually go unpunished and are often hidden from the general public and ignored by the government-controlled media.

The American press must also talk about the schoolteachers in sub-Sahara who work with so little and are often not even paid, compared to their counterparts elsewhere in the world. Some of the teachers still conduct classes under the trees instead of in classrooms. They lack textbooks, other basic materials, and all the essentials needed for doing their work. And yet they strive day after day to teach perhaps the most needy children in the world. These are the heroes of Africa whom the American people know very little about.

And of course there are the trade unionists and all the workers who labor under trying conditions with little or no pay. These workers are also heroes whom the America media should talk about.

The main focus here is to bring to Americans' attention the few positive things taking place in sub-Sahara. What we want most of all is for the American people to have confidence in the future of Africa. At this stage of development in sub-Sahara, everything seems to be utterly hopeless. And we must, to some extent, accept that judgment. The potential of Africa is there, and if that potential is properly nourished, then the rebirth of sub-Sahara will not be far behind.

The deep involvement of United States in those key areas of economic development has a superb chance of moving the poorest countries of Africa into a better position. The majority of the people on the continent would be most pleased to see the United States engaged in the economic reforms in their respective countries.

Some people in the United States are probably already tired of being called upon to help this or that country time and time again. But the case of sub-Sahara is very different, as I have discussed elsewhere. African history is also very different. Before the African continent was partitioned by European powers, there were no nation-states or countries as we know them today on the continent. After the partition, African countries endured many years of colonial domination, which left the peoples of Africa spiritually and mentally completely broken. The arrival of independence in the 1960s—granted to unprepared people—complicated matters for the new nations.

These African countries started off nationhood with nothing; we must be very frank about this point. Then came the wasted decades after political independence—wasted because the subcontinent didn't do much to transform itself or put in place concrete economic policies geared toward growth. The sub-Sahara didn't have a properly educated class of leaders to guide the newly independent countries in this brave new world; the leaders who rose to power were ushered in totally unprepared.

The sub-Sahara—yes, that backward region—is now at last looking forward, determined to correct past mistakes and work harder to create greater prosperity for its citizens in the twenty-first century and beyond. Some African countries are, fortunately, doing much better than others. Therefore, those countries that are trying the most deserve the support of the American people as the former continue to struggle for economic development and freedom. This level of support is definitely long overdue. Now that the hopes of millions of Africans in these countries have been raised, there is no turning back.

Africans, especially those who are young, are not going to sit idly by and let their countries descend back into the chaos and extreme poverty of the past. Therefore the call here is for the United States to help these countries to lay down solid foundations for sustained economic development, without which these countries will not successfully break the yoke of poverty and underdevelopment and all that comes with it.

7

The Involvement of US Faith-Based Organizations in Promoting Friendship between the United States and Africa

Up to this point, I have explored a few important ways that sub-Saharan Africa and the United States can bolster the mutual relationship between them for the long term. And to that list, I want to add the useful role that US churches can play to bring both sides together. Various US churches already have an extensive presence in sub-Sahara, and they are performing a lot of good works.

There is nothing more important than the relationship between these two regions solidified by faith, especially the common Christian heritage. Christians in the United States have a duty to see to it that their brothers and sisters in Africa also have a better future. The suffering of the majority in Africa has gone on for too long, and it has dealt a terrible blow to the confidence and morale of the African people.

The churches in the United States know too well about this suffering and that is why many of them are doing some kind of charity work in the region. And the citizens of the region are very grateful for all the assistance these faith-based groups are rendering to the poor, to the sick, to women, and to numerous other worthy humanitarian causes. However, it is now time to do more to empower the people of Africa so that they can stand firmly on their own two feet and hold the future of sub-Sahara in their hands.

Churches in the United States have a responsibility to work for the salvation and promotion of the bond between sub-Sahara and the United States. The kind of relationship I am talking about is a truly special one for the ages. Therefore, the total involvement of American faith-based organizations must be the foundation on which this new relationship is based. Some people, I am sure, believe that church organizations should not be at the forefront of expanding the relationship between the two partners.

I strongly beg to differ, because these US faith-based groups are in Africa to carry out charity work, which is significantly improving the lives of thousands of poor Africans. In addition, these groups are not in Africa with ulterior motives. They want what is generally best for the people there. As a result, it is perfectly proper for the US churches to make sure that Africa and the United States work together as true friends forever.

Interestingly, this kind of people-to-people relationship is extremely useful, because it greatly supplements the work of the diplomats and politicians who are sometimes known to fail in their duties. We have seen that happen again and again in regard to relations between the United States and Africa. We can no longer allow that to happen—not in the twenty-first century. The long-term future of Africa and its economic prosperity lies with Africa's closeness to the United States. This must be clearly stated and written because it is the truth. We must stop pretending the stakes are simply too high for both regions.

We want to encourage US faith-based groups to continue to

organize and provide, for example, more US doctors in various specialties to travel to Africa to provide high-quality medical care to the poor Africans in the villages. The level of medical care that American doctors—who are all volunteers—are giving to these Africans is superior to what they would ever receive in their respective countries, and most importantly, the services are all free of charge. Unfortunately, for the moment, these medical visits do not cover the entire sub-Saharan region. Therefore, it is the hope of all who care about the African people that US churches try to extend the visits to the entire region.

The provision of medical services is one of the critical lifesaving missions these American faith-based groups are undertaking in the mother continent. Luckily for the Africans, these groups are also performing other vital tasks, such as catering to the thousands of African children who are orphans because their parents died of HIV/ AIDS. Countless numbers of parents have died in the continent as a result of this deadly virus, and many have left their children in the care of the government, in the care of relatives, or simply abandoned. The problem is that the African governments are so disorganized that they are just not capable of taking care of these orphans. And it is even worse for the relatives, as most of them are very poor.

Consequently, a lot of these tasks are now being handled by outside groups, especially church groups in the United States. These missionaries provide funding for some of the orphanages and provide the basic necessities to children such as food and clothing, without which the children would probably not survive.

These basic social services are taken for granted in the United States but not in sub-Sahara. The situation there is dire, and the American churches know it all too well. The fact that they are doing something about these problems is a telling sign that they care a great deal about the African people.

What is impressive is that these church groups are using their own resources to provide all these important services. Do African governments even care that their citizens are depending on the American church groups and other NGOs for the basic services needed for their sustenance? Take, for example, the provision of clean water. In much of sub-Sahara, there are severe shortages of drinkable water. However, the African governments are not stepping up to meet the challenges of the water shortage.

Luckily, some US church groups have extensive experience in the provision of clean water in developing countries. I would therefore urge these groups to do more in the area of providing clean water. We are well aware of the dangers of consuming contaminated water.

Giving the African people the gift of clean water, medical care, and education, and sharing our and faith values, is the most hopeful thing in the relationship between Africa and the United States. US churches must do even more to urge American political and business leaders to think of Africa as a place of hope and opportunity. The two sides share so much in common and, therefore, should always work to foster the historic bonds so that this century turns out to be the best ever between Africa, the birthplace of humankind, and the United States—the greatest nation perhaps since the Roman Empire.

Conclusion

Cordial Relations between Africa and the United States in the Twenty-First Century: How the United States Can Help to Transform the Continent is about present and future relations between Africa and the United States. Some pessimists in both regions believe that it is virtually impossible for the two sides to have a meaningful relationship—especially now with the Trump administration. I don't believe so, for the simple reason that there is now too much at stake for both sides, as will be the case in the years to come.

Cordial Relations between Africa and the United States in the Twenty-First Century looks candidly at the complicated nature of the relationship and discusses how problematic it has been to overcome past problems and current misconceptions. However, the end of the rivalry between the Western democratic nations and the communist nations ushered in some fresh thinking and an opportunity for a new beginning between the two partners.

It is in this spirit that I urge the United States to use its vast reserve of resources and expertise to help the Africans build democratic institutions and strengthen their governance systems. Without these positive reforms, the continent will not realize its full potential for years to come.

Good governance will ultimately produce better economic and social results for the nations of Africa. As we have seen, poor economic performance in much of Africa is caused by the lack of efficient organization, the lack of security, and relatively poor education. The United States can help the continent to improve in these areas.

At the moment, too many obstacles are standing in the way for foreign companies to make investments in Africa. As discussed in *Cordial Relations between Africa and the United States in the Twenty-First Century,* one of those obstacles is general security. The insecurity in Africa makes it extremely hard for any country to make serious progress there. Here again is where the United States can assist, helping African nations to improve their security systems. The United States Africa Command should be at forefront of this effort.

The United States' generous response to Africa's HIV/AIDS epidemic shall always be remembered by the citizens of the continent. I personally know of many people, including some of my best friends, who perished from this disease. The intervention of the United States, with a major assistance plan, greatly helped to slow the spread of HIV/AIDS in the continent.

In the 1960s, the United States cooperated fairly extensively with most African nations when it came to education and culture. This US policy led to substantial US investment in Africa's schools. In Uganda, for example, the United States built secondary schools and helped out institutions of higher learning. This is the kind of help Africa still needs from the United States.

In recent years, US nongovernmental organizations, especially faith-based groups, have significantly increased their humanitarian activities in the continent. I highly welcome their participation in the region and hope that church groups will double their efforts in critical areas, such as the provision of clean water, education, health care, and nutrition and the assisting of persons displaced on account of the civil conflicts in some countries.

When President Obama was traveling within Africa, specifically to the countries of Senegal, South Africa, and Tanzania, he called for a new partnership between Africa and the United States. He went on to say that this partnership should be based on trade and not aid, as has traditionally been the case. The president should be applauded for reaffirming this yet undefined policy related to the relationship between the two regions. We must, however, keep in mind that trade and private sector investments from the United States have not been growing in sub-Sahara for decades. This is not about to change now—and for a very good reason.

If US presidents want to see more direct foreign investments (DFI) into sub-Sahara, then the first thing to do is to help these countries to rebuild their infrastructure, that is, roads, rail lines, airports, bridges, and shipping facilities. The following may come as a shock to many people outside Africa, but it is true. Some African countries have not built or improved on their general infrastructure since the European colonialists left the continent in the 1960s. Most of the roads and rail lines built during the colonial era have all disappeared, or else they were just left to crumble as the subregion was taken over by political instability and violent conflicts, which are still with us today in some countries.

Then you have the shortage of electricity. The majority of the sub-Saharan countries are not producing enough power right now. Only the Republic of South Africa has the capacity to produce the power it needs for economic growth. All other sub-Saharan nations are struggling with perennial power shortages—a situation that is not going to improve without a massive amount of help from a country like the USA. Only the United States, with its track record of nation building and its sheer economic power, is capable of helping these countries reform and rebuild their infrastructure. Without US intervention, along with the necessary resources, the future of much of sub-Sahara is bleak indeed. Africa's foreseeable future depends on US intervention.

Let us stop kidding ourselves. If you think the situation is not that alarming in the greater part of the region, then visit countries such as the Congo (DRC), South Sudan, and Zimbabwe, where you will see some extreme situations. Some people, perhaps, think that this is an exaggeration of the African state of affairs. I only wish it were an exaggeration. The truth is that it is not. The people of sub-Saharan Africa have never experienced a higher quality of life with regard to the economy, the social situation, national security, health care, and other things happily enjoyed and taken for granted elsewhere in the world, especially in the United States.

We want exactly the same prosperity for sub-Sahara. Why not? Why should the world always have such a low expectation for Africa? It is time for some African countries, and I mean those countries that are genuinely making heroic efforts to better themselves, to stand up and say that they reject this perpetual characterization of Africa.

Unfortunately, even with a massive amount of assistance and goodwill from the United States, only a few sub-Saharan nations will truly emerge from economic underdevelopment in our lifetime! This is because they are so far behind and so disorganized that it will take probably another century for them to join the ranks of prosperous nations, even among other African states.

As already mentioned in this chapter, there are a few countries in the sub-Sahara that have been trying to improve living conditions for their citizens, with surprisingly modest successes. At the top in this respect is the Republic of South Africa, followed by Botswana, Kenya, Mauritius, Uganda, Senegal, Ghana, and a few others scattered across the region. For example, the modest progress that has been made in Uganda over the last two decades or so is short of a miracle, considering the fact that this small landlocked East African nation once had been completely written off. But now this once sick nation has made a spectacular recovery, with the help of the United States and other developed countries in the West. The recovery is not yet complete, but there is hope.

President Museveni has set up an ambitious goal of turning Uganda into a middle-income country by 2017! What this means is that he wants Uganda to become like Singapore, Malaysia, India, or Hong Kong—in just five years from now. Is this really an achievable goal for this poor country? The problem for Museveni is that he has not invested enough capital in the building of the much needed infrastructure and other critical projects that are a prerequisite for such a huge degree of economic modernization. For Uganda to become a middle-income country by 2017, it must, for example, start to generate enough income on its own to cover the country's national budget. In addition, it must modernize its general infrastructure, build more power plants to provide electricity for the whole country, make sure that the country has a sufficient educated and flexible workforce, and eliminate illiteracy in the country. If President Museveni can accomplish some of these things with the help of the United States, he will have achieved the impossible and, perhaps, his dream of 2017 could also be accomplished.

But it is sad to say that the prospects are not good for President Museveni, for the simple reason that Uganda and Africa in general have a poor track record of growing their economies. Even countries with enormous oil wealth, such as Angola, Nigeria, Equatorial Guinea, and Gabon, are nowhere near middle-income nations. These oil-rich countries are just as poor as the other sub-Saharan countries. The poverty is endemic in sub-Sahara, in spite of its abundant natural resources, which African nations have been producing and exporting since independence in the 1960s. Today these countries have nothing to show to the world as concrete proof that they have invested their oil resources well and that they are on their way to changing the economic status quo in the region.

That is why, this time, something different ought to be attempted for the sake of the suffering masses in sub-Sahara. The appeal to the US government to put its economic might behind this struggle is the only viable and promising way forward. The US government, just like with the HIV/AIDS epidemic, should come up with a solid economic plan, like the Marshall Plan, aimed at those countries in sub-Sahara with a demonstrated record of economic reform and generally good governance. Countries such as Ethiopia, Uganda, Rwanda, Botswana, Senegal, Tanzania, Ghana, and Mauritius have the potential to become the next Singapore, Malaysia, Hong Kong, Taiwan, India, or even China—but this time in sub-Saharan Africa.

US companies have largely stayed out of sub-Sahara because there is nothing there to attract them to the region. No company wants to invest its precious capital in a country with no proper roads, poor education, corrupt government, inadequate power, no laws for protecting private property, and involvement in constant political conflicts. Unfortunately, this is the true state of affairs in sub-Sahara. These are enormous problems that African countries, with the help of the United States, must deal with if the region ever wants to become the next economic success.

Singapore, a tiny Asian country, is an economic success partly because it has managed to attract, for example, a large number of American and European companies to invest in it. It is said that these American companies have invested well over US$100 billion into Singapore. What is important here is that Singapore and other successful Asian countries have all the fundamentals in place. Therefore, the foreign investors are confident that they can safely put their capital into these countries.

And that is what it will take to attract these wealthy investors to sub-Sahara. Those countries in Africa such as Uganda with ambitions of joining the ranks of the richer nations in the near future must continue to prepare the groundwork for eventually achieving that goal. Ghana, Uganda, Rwanda, Senegal, Mauritius, Kenya, and a few others must be congratulated for striving to become rich modern entities in a sea of hopelessness and depression.

However, as already noted, the odds are very must against them, unless, of course, they manage to engage and attract everything that the United States has to offer, especially the values that have made it one of the most successful nations in the history of the world. Solid economic and political success in one or more countries in sub-Saharan Africa would be extremely good for the entire region. This time Africa must have the United States on its side.

Printed in the United States
By Bookmasters